It's another Quality Book from CGP

This book is for anyone studying OCR GCSE Textiles.

It explains all the technical details you'll need to understand, with plenty of full-colour diagrams to help make everything crystal-clear.

We've also included advice to help make your project a winner, plus tips on how to improve your exam technique.

What CGP is all about

Our sole aim here at CGP is to produce the highest quality books — carefully written, immaculately presented and dangerously close to being funny.

Then we work our socks off to get them out to you — at the cheapest possible prices.

Contents

SECTION THREE — TOOLS AND PROCESSES

SECTION FOUR — MARKET INFLUENCES

SECTION FIVE — INDUSTRIAL AWARENESS

Published by CGP

Editors:
Charlotte Burrows, Ben Fletcher, Rosie Gillham, David Hickinson, John Kitching,
Adam Moorhouse, Ali Palin, Dave Ryan, Julie Wakeling, Sarah Williams.

Contributors:
Anne Ainsworth, Nicole Billinge and Sue Carrington.

With thanks to Kelly Rogers for the content review.
With thanks to Simon Little and Charlotte Tweedy for the proofreading.

ISBN: 978 1 84762 350 8

With thanks to Laura Stoney for the copyright research.

With thanks to Science Photo Library for permission to use the image on page 13.

With thanks to Australian Wool Innovation Limited for permission to reproduce the Woolmark logo on page 68.

With thanks to www.care-labelling.co.uk for permission to use the European Textile Care Labels on page 68.

With thanks to The British Toy & Hobby Association for permission to reproduce the Lion Mark logo on page 58.

With thanks to iStockphoto® for permission to use the image on page 41.

With thanks to BSI for permission to reproduce the Kitemark symbol on page 58. Kitemark and the Kitemark symbol are registered trademarks of BSI. For more information visit www.kitemark.com.

GORE-TEX®, GORE® and designs are registered trade marks of W L Gore & Associates.

Every effort has been made to locate copyright holders and obtain permission to reproduce sources.
For those sources where it has been difficult to trace the originator of the work, we would be grateful
for information. If any copyright holder would like us to make an amendment to the acknowledgements,
please notify us and we will gladly update the book at the next reprint. Thank you.

Clipart from Corel®
Printed by Elanders Ltd, Newcastle upon Tyne.

Based on the classic CGP style created by Richard Parsons.

Project Advice

Unlike most subjects, in Textiles you actually get to make something trendy (well, hopefully).

The Projects are Worth 60% of your GCSE

1) Your Textiles projects are called 'controlled assessments'.

2) There are two projects — the first one is about designing and making a prototype, and the other one is about designing and making a quality product. Each project is worth 60 marks.

3) Your teacher will give you as much help as they're allowed to by the exam board, so do ask them... but mostly it's up to you to make a good job of your projects.

4) You can dip into this book for a bit of extra help. Section One is all about the design process, so if you're not sure where to start, that might be a good place to look.

5) If you're wondering about a particular detail — the properties of cotton, say — it's probably quickest to look that up in the index and go straight to that page.

The Exam Board Sets the Themes

You'll be given a range of themes and starting points to choose from for your projects.

> For example: An animal-themed textile product that will appeal to young children.

Remember — you've got to pick a different theme for each of your projects.

Only Put Relevant Stuff in Your Folder

1) Your teacher will give you plenty of guidance on what needs to go in your folder, but you can use this section of the book for a reminder.

2) The next two pages tell you what you can get marks for and give you a few tips on how to get them.

3) Include plenty of detail — but don't waffle and don't waste space on irrelevant stuff.

Include Plenty of Photos

1) DO put in lots of photos. You MUST take at least two photos of your final product — a front view and a back view. (You might also want to include a photo of, say, the inside of a bag to show the jazzy lining and pockets.)

2) But also, take photos while you're developing your design (see next page)...

3) ...and during the intermediate stages of making your product, to show the making process.

Example

The fastenings need to be strong, so I'm using metal zips. It doesn't matter that they are bulky because denim is a heavy fabric.

The pockets are attached using double stitching to provide extra strength.

Controlled Assessment — nope, it's not funny...

Most of the controlled assessment marks depend on the sheer brilliance of your folder, so don't worry if you're not the next Ms. Prada — you'll get loads of marks for explaining what you're making and why.

Project Advice

The first project needs to show the moderator how you've got from the starting point to your prototype.

Cultural Understanding is Worth 5 Marks

1) Show that you understand how culture and society affect textile products — and how products can influence culture and society (e.g. materials, styles and methods of making products).
2) Think about how textile products can help to improve people's lifestyles and choices — see page 4.

Creativity is Worth 5 Marks

1) Research existing products — visit shops to research materials, get ideas from magazines or the internet.
2) Identify and research your target market — find out what they need and want, so will be more likely to buy.
3) Analyse your research — summarise your findings and say how they'll influence your design.
4) Look at trends in existing products — materials used, styles, etc. and take these into account when designing your product.

Designing is Worth 14 Marks

1) Write a detailed design specification (see page 10) — based on your design brief and research analysis.
2) Come up with a range of creative and original ideas to meet your design specification.
3) Present your design ideas clearly. Annotate (add notes to) your drawings so it's clear what materials will be used and how they'll be fixed together, etc. Use ICT to help you — see pages 12-13 for more info.
4) Test out your ideas by making models and record your results — take photos.
5) Choose your best design idea — the one that most closely matches the design specification.

Making is Worth 28 Marks

1) Plan your time and organise yourself well — e.g. you could make a flowchart to show the order of tasks.
2) Use the most appropriate materials to make your product — think about the pros and cons of the different materials and components you could use, their effects on the environment, how much they cost, etc.
3) Select the most suitable hand and machine tools to use, and explain your reasons.
4) Work accurately and skilfully, using the right techniques and tools for the job — use CAM if appropriate.
5) Work safely — think about the risks and show that you've minimised them.
6) Record the key stages involved in making your product — write detailed notes as well as taking photos.
7) Don't worry if problems spring up along the way — you'll get marks for identifying and solving them.

Evaluating is Worth 8 Marks

1) This is all about critically evaluating the process used to make your prototype (picking out the good and bad points). What went well? What worked and what didn't? What would you change and why?
2) Your prototype is unlikely to be perfect, so suggest some improvements you could make to it.
3) Use specialist terms — but only if you know what they mean (use the glossary on pages 76-77).
4) Double check your spelling, grammar and punctuation to make sure you don't lose out on marks.

Tell the story of your design — and give it a happy ending...

You'd scarcely believe how much moderators hate wading through pages and pages of designs that you've copied from magazines or off the internet. So do your research — then develop your own original ideas.

Project Advice

Your <u>second project</u> needs to show in detail how you've <u>designed</u> and <u>made</u> a quality product.
The marks you get are pretty similar to the first project — but the focus is more on your <u>final product</u>.

Designing is Worth 16 Marks

1) Produce a detailed <u>design specification</u> based on the design brief and your research.
2) Come up with a range of creative and well-presented <u>design ideas</u> — Use <u>ICT</u> and <u>CAD</u> to help you.
3) <u>Clearly</u> show all the details of the design you're going to make, and use <u>models</u> to work out the best way to <u>make</u> it.

Making is Worth 36 Marks

Shelley was very excited about getting to model the two-handbag design.

1) <u>Plan</u>, <u>organise</u> and <u>record</u> the making process — *write detailed notes, do some annotated drawings and take lots of photos.*
2) Use the most appropriate <u>materials</u>, <u>components</u>, <u>tools</u> and <u>equipment</u> — *and give reasons for your choices.*
3) Show that you know about ICT, CAM, different production systems and quality control when you're making your product.
4) Work <u>skilfully</u> and <u>safely</u> to make a quality product. *Don't be slapdash, it'll show.*
5) Remember to take lots of <u>photos</u>, especially of your final product — *take photos from different angles and show what your product looks like when it's actually being used, e.g. you could get someone to model your product.*
6) Remember, <u>don't worry</u> about <u>problems</u>, you'll get marks for <u>solving them</u>.

Evaluating is Worth 8 Marks

1) Do some serious <u>testing</u> of your product — get people to use it
   — e.g. get someone to take your bag when they go shopping and see how well it works.
2) <u>Critically evaluate</u> your finished product (pick out good and bad points). What went well? What would you change and why?
3) Present your information in a <u>clear</u> and <u>structured</u> way
   — plan what you're going to write and use ICT to help you.
4) Make sure you <u>explain things clearly</u> — get someone who knows nothing about your project to read it and see if it <u>makes sense</u>.
5) Moderators love it when you use the right <u>technical words</u>
   — they love it even more when you spell them correctly.

Make sure your conclusions say something useful about your product — don't just fill space with a load of waffle.

But Don't Forget The Exam — It's Worth 40%

1) There is one exam which will test you on <u>everything</u> you've learned during the course — materials, tools, how to design things, how to make things, health and safety, environmental issues...
2) This book can help you <u>learn all that stuff</u> — and it has <u>questions</u> for you to <u>check</u> what you know.
3) There's a <u>glossary</u> at the back of the book, in case you need to sort out your microfibres from your micro-encapsulation.
4) The <u>exam technique</u> section (pages 72-75) has some <u>worked examples</u> of exam-style questions, and some hints on how to make sure you get <u>top marks</u>.

Evaaaaaaal-u-ate good times, come on...

When you evaluate a design or product, remember to explain <u>which aspects</u> of the design or product need changing and <u>why</u>. It's another little step on the long and winding road to coursework heaven.

Design Issues

Designing isn't as simple as it sounds — there are loads of things to think about...

Good Product Designs **Can** Improve Quality of Life

Quality of life describes a person's social, emotional and physical well-being. Well designed textile products can improve a person's quality of life by being easy to use, functional (doing what they're meant to do) and aesthetically pleasing (looking good).

> For example, a waterproof coat is functional if it keeps you dry when it rains — this improves the user's physical well-being because they don't get cold and wet. A dress looks good if it has a good style and a nice colour — this can improve a user's social/emotional well-being by making them more confident.

Product choice can also improve quality of life — the more products there are on the market the more likely it is that a consumer will find one that meets their needs.

Designers Respond **to** Outside Influences

In order for their products to sell, designers need to take into account these factors in their designs:

CHANGING STYLES
Style is influenced by fashion trends — when fashions follow a particular direction, e.g. military jackets, goth features. Fashion trends are constantly changing and designers have to keep up-to-date with them by looking at fashion forecast websites and attending fashion shows.

TECHNOLOGICAL ADVANCES
New fabrics can improve a product's functionality and appearance, e.g. smart fabrics (see pages 28-29) are used in fashion t-shirts. As other new technologies, like mobile phones, become popular people expect them to be incorporated into designs, e.g. mobile phone pockets in bags.

ENVIRONMENTAL PRESSURES
The textile industry has a huge impact on the environment (see p.60-61) and many consumers are worried about this. Designers can make their products more appealing by making them more environmentally-friendly (see below).

TASTE
People's taste is what they like. This is influenced by fashion trends, age and lifestyle. Designers can carry out market research (see p.9) to find out what their target market likes.

Eco-design **is** Better **for the** Environment

For more on environmental issues see pages 60-61.

Eco-design is designing a product that has a low impact on the environment throughout its life. To do this a designer has to look at the whole life cycle of a product and minimise the environmental damage at each stage. For example:

RAW MATERIALS
- Choose materials from renewable sources.
- Choose materials that use minimal energy in processing.

MANUFACTURE
- Minimise energy use.
- Minimise waste.
- Minimise use of harmful substances.

DISTRIBUTION
- Use energy-efficient transportation.
- Have factory close to market.

USE
- Minimise energy use required in maintenance (e.g. washing).

DISPOSAL
- Design so easy to recycle.
- Use biodegradable materials.

Lots of bags and shoes definitely improve my quality of life...

Product design is more important than you think — a good product can do wonders for our well-being and be kind to the planet too. Make sure you learn all the factors that can affect product design.

Design Issues

Textile Products _are_ Made _and_ Sold Globally

1) Before there were good transport and communication links, most products were designed, manufactured and sold in the same country.

2) Now it's common for products to be designed in one country, manufactured in another, and then sold all over the world. This is known as globalisation.

3) Companies may choose to manufacture their products abroad due to:

- Cheaper raw materials
- Cheaper labour costs
- Greater availability of workers
- Workforce having specialist skills (e.g. sewing)
- Lower overheads (e.g. rent)

4) Some products are made in more than one country. For example, the components for a bag (e.g. zips) may be bought from different countries before being assembled in one place.

5) The globalisation of products has advantages and disadvantages:

Advantages

- Production costs are lower because materials can be sourced from where they're cheapest and taken for processing to countries where wages and energy are cheap.
- The savings made during production may be passed on to consumers as lower prices.
- Consumers have greater product choice — there are more raw materials, colours and designs available, e.g. Indian silks can be used to design and make new products for the European market. Also, consumers can buy products from all over the world in high street stores or directly over the internet.
- Manufacturers can sell their products worldwide, making more money.

Designers now have access to fabrics from all over the world.

Disadvantages

- More energy is used and more pollution is created because materials, parts and finished products are transported from country to country.
- Designing can become more complicated — e.g. products designed to be sold worldwide need to take into account many different cultures (see p.57).
- Some people think that globalisation reduces the variety of design, with products from different places and cultures becoming more and more similar.
- Companies may use factories abroad to take advantage of cheap labour (see above). However, this means that products designed and sold in Britain may be made in factories abroad that have poor working conditions (see p.59).

Practice Questions

1) Explain, using examples, how a textile product can improve a person's:
   a) social/emotional wellbeing.
   b) physical wellbeing.

2) Give four factors that influence designers when they create a design.

3) What is eco-design?

4) Globalisation means many companies manufacture and sell their products in different countries.
   a) Give three advantages of globalisation.
   b) Give three disadvantages of globalisation.

Product Analysis

Before designing a new product it's a good idea to look at other products on the market...

Product Analysis Can Give You Ideas For Your Design

If you need an idea for a product, you can use product analysis to see what's already on the market and what's not (gaps in the market). Once you've got your design brief (see p.8) you can analyse a variety of similar products to help you with your own design.

If you wanted to design a reusable shopping bag, you could start by looking at ones already on the market.

Product analysis is carried out by looking carefully at the outside of a product (this may be easier if the garment is on a mannequin) or by disassembling it (taking the product apart, see below). You need to consider the following factors:

FUNCTION AND FITNESS FOR PURPOSE: Function is what the product is intended to do. The type of fabric might give an idea of this, e.g. sportswear is designed to be worn when playing sports, so will be made of fabric that is light and breathable. Fitness for purpose is how well the product can do this function. To find out whether a product is fit for purpose you need to test it (see next page), e.g. if it's a waterproof coat you need to wear it in the rain.

TARGET MARKET: Try to work out what group of people the product is aimed at. You can often tell this from the product's aesthetics (appearance), its ergonomics (see p.14) and price. E.g. cheaper clothes that are fashionable, but made out of thinner fabrics with poor stitching quality are likely to be aimed at young people who don't have a lot of money.

MATERIALS AND COMPONENTS: Work out what fibres and fabrics, fastenings and other pre-manufactured components have been used — the product labelling might help you with this. Think about why they were used — look at what properties they have (see pages 24-25 and 38-39). For example, a bag aimed at young people is made out of polyurethane. This synthetic material is cheaper than leather, comes in different colours and is stiff so it holds its shape — these properties all make it suitable for its function and target group.

MANUFACTURE: You should also consider the processes that have been used to make the product. This can be done by disassembly — taking a product apart (unpicking it) allows you to see the shape of the original garment pieces and gives you information on:

- Pattern layout.
- Types of fabrics, linings and interfacings used.
- Types of pre-manufactured components used and how they're attached.
- Construction techniques used.
- Decorative techniques used.
- Order the pieces were put together in.

I buy lots of clothes, purely for product analysis reasons...

Product analysis gives you lots of useful information about products already on the market. You can use this information to design new products that people will want, instead of the same old thing...

Product Analysis

The next step on from analysing a product is to <u>test</u> it out.

Test Products to Find Out How to Improve the Designs

1) You can test a product to <u>check</u> that it's <u>fit for purpose</u>. <u>Using</u> the product in the <u>way it was designed to be used</u> helps to check that it actually <u>does what it's supposed to do</u> — e.g. loading a reusable shopping bag with shopping, putting up a tent, trying on a dress.

2) Features that affect a product's fitness for purpose, like <u>size</u>, <u>ease of use</u>, <u>fastenings</u> and <u>durability</u> can be evaluated more rigorously by <u>testing</u> it rather than by just looking at it (see previous page). E.g. a reusable shopping bag may look big enough, but might not actually hold a lot of shopping when tested.

3) Testing products might give you ideas for improvements to include in your own design, to make it <u>more appealing</u> to the consumer, so it will <u>sell</u>. You might be able to improve:

- The <u>design</u> itself — <u>innovation</u> in design is designing a product that is <u>new</u> or <u>different</u>. Identifying a product or part of it that doesn't fit its purpose can <u>help generate new design ideas</u> that <u>satisfy the consumer's needs</u>. E.g. a tent might be waterproof in light storms but not in heavy storms, so designing a tent that survives heavy storms could <u>fill a gap in the market</u>.

- The <u>materials</u> and <u>processes</u> — e.g. a white polyamide/LYCRA® mix might seem like a good fabric for a swimming costume because it's stretchy and dries quickly, but on testing it may become see-through when wet — this design could be <u>improved</u> by <u>changing the colour</u> of the fabric used.

You Can Make a Product More Sustainable

You could improve an existing product by making it <u>more sustainable</u> — this means <u>more environmentally friendly</u>. When <u>analysing</u> or <u>testing</u> the product think about the effect it has on the environment — from its <u>raw materials</u> to its <u>disposal</u>. Then think of ways you could make the product more sustainable, for example:

ANALYSIS OF A DYED POLYESTER BLOUSE

Environmental problems	Improvements to the design
• <u>Huge amount of energy</u> used to make polyester.	• Make blouse out of <u>natural fibres</u>.
• <u>Heat/water wasted</u> during manufacturing process.	• <u>Reuse heat/water</u> in manufacturing process.
• <u>Toxic dye</u> released in waste water.	• Use <u>non-toxic dyes</u> or <u>clean</u> wastewater.
• Thrown away in <u>landfill</u>.	• Make blouse out of <u>biodegradable</u> fabric.

Practice Questions

1) Sue wants to design a hat. She starts by analysing hats by another designer.
   a) Give <u>two</u> advantages for Sue of doing this.
   b) Suggest <u>three</u> features Sue could look at when analysing the hats.
   c) <u>Why</u> might it help her to <u>disassemble</u> the other designer's hats?

2) John makes waterproof jackets. He wants to <u>test</u> his latest design to see if it is fit for purpose.
   a) Explain what is meant by '<u>fitness for purpose</u>'.
   b) Suggest how John could <u>test</u> his design.
   c) From the tests, John decides to change the <u>design</u> of his product. Suggest <u>another factor</u> he might be able to change to improve his product.

Task Analysis and Research

The process of <u>designing</u> and <u>making</u> something is called '<u>the design process</u>' (oooooooh). Here's how it all starts...

First There Needs to be an Idea for a New Product

Someone must come up with an <u>idea</u> for a <u>new textiles product</u>. Lots of things can spark off the idea for a new product, such as:

1) <u>Problems</u> with an existing product.
2) <u>Improvements</u> to the <u>performance</u> of an existing design.
3) A <u>gap</u> in the market.

Product analysis (see pages 6-7) can help develop initial ideas into a specific product.

A Design Brief Introduces the Idea for a New Product

Once an idea has been thought of, a <u>design brief</u> must be written. This is a <u>statement</u> for the <u>designer</u> describing the <u>initial task</u>. It'll probably include:

1) an <u>outline</u> of the <u>context</u> (background) and <u>who</u> the product is aimed at (the target group)
2) what <u>kind</u> of product is needed and <u>why</u>
3) how the product will be <u>used</u>

Design Brief
A specialist tie shop sells many different types of ties. Currently there are no sports-themed ties. Design and make a tie for a golf fan which could be sold in the shop.

The design brief is <u>short</u> and to-the-point — it's a <u>starting point</u> for the <u>development</u> of the product. The <u>designer</u> needs to meet the design brief in terms of the <u>function</u> and <u>aesthetics</u> of the product:

FUNCTION

The function of a product is <u>how</u> it will be <u>used</u> and this is usually given in the <u>design brief</u>. To fulfil its function the product needs to <u>do what it's meant to do</u>, be <u>easy to manufacture</u>, <u>work efficiently</u>, <u>enhance the user's image</u>, <u>look good</u> and be <u>saleable</u>.

AESTHETICS

The aesthetics of a product is its <u>look</u> or <u>appearance</u>. Aesthetics includes the <u>style</u> of the product and <u>properties</u> such as <u>drape</u>, <u>colour</u>, <u>texture</u> and <u>decoration</u>.

Research is an Important Part of the Design Process

The next step is to do some <u>research</u> — this should include <u>product analysis</u> to find out what's already on the market, and to get <u>information</u> and <u>inspiration</u> for your own designs. You also need to do some <u>market research</u> (see next page) to find out what the target group wants. <u>ICT</u> can help you <u>research</u> and <u>present</u> this information:

1) You could use a <u>database</u> to keep details about products you've <u>analysed</u>, including the <u>fabrics</u> etc. that were used. You could also take <u>photos</u> of the products using a <u>digital camera</u> and upload them to the database.

2) You could write a <u>questionnaire</u> using <u>word processing</u> software — so it'll be <u>neat</u> and easy to read. You could post it on a <u>website</u> that your <u>target group</u> is likely to use, so they could fill it in <u>online</u>.

3) You could use <u>spreadsheets</u> to <u>organise and sort data</u> (e.g. your questionnaire results). Spreadsheets also allow you to <u>present</u> the data using <u>charts</u> and <u>graphs</u>.

Shopping is my favourite type of textile research...

Whether in industry or at school, the design process <u>always starts</u> with an <u>idea</u>, a <u>design brief</u> and lots of <u>research</u>. So I'm off to do some research into furry knickers — I reckon there's a gap in the market.

Task Analysis and Research

As well as <u>researching products</u>, you need to find out what people <u>want to buy</u> — this is called <u>market research</u>.

Identify Your Target Group and Ask Them Questions

Even the very best products won't be everyone's cup of tea — some people will <u>like</u> them, some <u>won't</u>. The people who are <u>most likely</u> to buy your product should be clear from your design brief — they're your <u>target group</u>. Ask members of your target group <u>what they want</u> the product to be like. You could find out:

1) Some information about the <u>person</u> answering your questions. This could help you make sure they're within your <u>target group</u>, or give you <u>extra information</u>.

2) Do they already <u>buy</u> the kind of product you're thinking of developing?

3) Do they like a particular <u>style</u> or <u>colour</u>?

4) <u>How much</u> would they be prepared to pay for this kind of product? This could affect your <u>budget</u> — the lower the selling price, the lower the manufacturing costs will need to be to make a profit.

5) <u>Where</u> would they expect to buy it from? Again, this could affect costs. E.g. if the majority of your target group buy from low-budget retailers, e.g. Primark®, you should design a low-cost product.

6) Is there something they <u>would like</u> from the product that existing products <u>don't have</u>?

Beth's target group had lots of opinions on what type of stripy trousers she should design...

You could present these questions in a:

Questionnaire — a <u>form</u> for people to fill in. Questions can be:

- <u>Closed</u> questions — these have a <u>limited</u> number of possible answers, e.g. '<u>do you ever use a bag?</u>' can only be answered 'YES' or 'NO'. Analysing is easy and you can show clear results at the end.

- <u>Open</u> questions — these have <u>no set answers</u>, e.g. <u>what's your favourite type of bag, and why?</u> They give people a chance to provide details and opinions.

Interview — a <u>face-to-face conversation</u>.

For interviews, you can <u>start off</u> by asking the same sort of questions as in questionnaires — but then take the chance to ask <u>follow-up</u> questions, based on the answers you get. Get your interviewees to give you <u>extra information</u> to explain their answer — this might help you get more <u>ideas</u> for your product. E.g. if their favourite hat is a beret, ask them <u>why</u> they like it.

Practice Questions

1) Samantha has been given a <u>design brief</u> to design some pants.
   a) What is a <u>design brief</u>? Suggest <u>three</u> things it could include.
   b) Give <u>two</u> ways that Samantha's product must meet the design brief.

2) Give <u>three</u> ways a student could use <u>ICT</u> to help them research and present data.

3) You are designing a <u>babygrow</u> and want to do some <u>research</u>.
   a) Who is your <u>target group</u>?
   b) You go to a parent and baby group to talk to the <u>parents</u>.
   Think of <u>three useful questions</u> you could <u>ask them</u> about the babygrows <u>they buy</u>.

4) a) Jordan plans to <u>interview</u> people for her market research. She wants to ask them <u>whether</u> they'd buy flip-flops and what <u>sizes</u> and <u>colours</u> they'd want. Peter says using a <u>questionnaire</u> to get the answers to these questions might be better. <u>Is Peter right</u>? Explain <u>why</u>.
   b) Jordan decides to broaden her questions to ask about <u>what sort</u> of beach shoes people <u>like</u>, and <u>why</u>. Describe the <u>potential benefits</u> and <u>drawbacks</u> of using this <u>type of question</u>.

Design Specification and Proposals

In order to find out what all your research means for your product, you need to...

Draw Conclusions From Your Research

Research gives you loads of information. Now it's time to use it — this is called research analysis:

1) Summarise what you've found out — pick out the most important and useful findings.
2) Explain what impact the research will have on your designs.
3) Suggest ways forward from the research you've done.

Then Write a Design Specification

1) The conclusions from your research should show what kind of characteristics your product must have.

2) Write up these characteristics as a detailed list of design criteria. This list is called a design specification.

3) You should include points to cover some or all of the following:

- aesthetics (shape, size, colour, etc.)
- function (how it will be used)
- financial constraints
- safety issues
- theme
- target market
- fabrics (i.e. properties & features)
- components (zips, buttons, etc.)
- construction & decorative techniques

4) Each point says one thing about what the product should be like.
E.g.

> Design Specification for a Reusable Shopping Bag
> - The finished bag must be retailed for £3 or less.
> - It must appeal to young people.
> - It must be made out of environmentally-friendly material.
> - It must be brightly-coloured.
> - It must be strong enough to hold shopping.
> - It must be machine washable.
> - It must fold down to fit into another bag.
> - It must be suitable for mass production.
> - It must have a secure pocket.   Etc...

"You could make a bag just like mine. (Just don't tell anyone the handle broke)."

EXAM TIP
In the exam, you might be given a specification and asked to design something to fit it.

5) The criteria must be related to your research — don't just make them up because they sound good.

6) The design specification is a starting point from which you can generate your design ideas.

7) Throughout the design process you'll need to refer back to the design specification and evaluate your product designs against it. The final product design must meet all the specification points.

There are a Few Tricks that Can Help You Get Started

Coming up with creative ideas can be daunting so try one of the following:

1) You could create a mood board — lots of different images, words, fabrics etc. that might trigger ideas for a design.
2) Work from an existing product — change some of its features or production methods so that it fits your design criteria.
3) Or you could do a spot of brainstorming (see the next page).

Brainstorm — no lightning but hopefully some striking ideas

Mood boards, existing products and brainstorms can help you generate your first ideas — but make sure you keep thinking of the design specification as you go because your final design idea must fit it.

Design Specification and Proposals

As I was saying, brainstorming is a great way to get your creative juices flowing...

Brainstorm to Produce Some Ideas

The outcome of a successful brainstorm for casual weekend-wear...

1) First, think up key words, questions and initial thoughts relating to your product. Use the design specification criteria to guide you.

2) Don't be too critical at this stage — let your imagination run wild. Even if an idea sounds ridiculous, put it down anyway. Be creative and get as many ideas as you can.

3) Afterwards, decide which ones are good (and so are worth developing) and which ones are as stupid as a holey umbrella.

4) You might want to combine the best features from a few of your ideas to generate a really good idea. E.g. looking at the brainstorm below, the heart bag may be popular with young people, but the stripy cotton bag may be more practical — so you could have a cotton bag with a heart motif... lovely.

You can do quick sketches as you brainstorm.

Key words:
foldable young bright
environment cheap
pocket strong

Questions:
How can it be light AND strong?
Can plastic be environmentally-friendly?
What kind of patterns are popular with young people?

Red, heart-shaped bag with side zip

Thick plastic bag with clear pockets for photos

Large blue hemp bag with flower pattern — folds in half

IDEAS FOR A REUSABLE SHOPPING BAG

Stripy A4 cotton bag with cord handles

Purple net bag — fully foldable

Pet kangaroo — use its pouch when shopping

Practice Questions

1) Describe the three-step process you'd use to draw conclusions from your research.

2) Suggest five things you should consider when writing a design specification.

3) What's a mood board and what's it used for?

4) You are briefed to design a CGP tea towel. Suggest five design criteria.

5) You're asked to design two new products.
For each one below, suggest why the given method is a sensible way to come up with initial ideas.
a) A lighter and more fashionable rucksack for day trips — work from existing products.
b) Quilt covers and pillowcases inspired by Art Deco and 1920s fashions — use a mood board.

Generating Design Ideas

Now you need to <u>sort</u> your <u>good ideas</u> from your bad ones, <u>sketch</u> them out and <u>develop</u> them. Easy.

You Need to Come Up with a Range of Initial Ideas

1) You'll need to present <u>more than one</u> design that <u>meets</u> the <u>design criteria</u> — both in the <u>exam</u> and for your <u>projects</u>.

2) When <u>presenting</u> your ideas, it's usually best to keep it simple — a <u>freehand</u> <u>pencil sketch</u> will do fine, as long as it's <u>clear</u> and <u>neat</u>.

3) If you're <u>confident</u>, you could try something a bit posher, like a 3D drawing.

4) It's important that you think you could actually <u>make</u> your design ideas — don't go overboard on exciting ideas that you could never produce for real.

5) <u>Annotate</u> (i.e. add <u>notes</u> to) each design idea to fully <u>explain</u> what it is and why it's <u>good</u>. You could mention the fabrics, colours, shape, decorative/construction techniques etc.

Design Ideas for a Reusable Shopping Bag
First Idea

Organic cotton fabric — this is strong, environmentally-friendly and foldable

Brightly coloured, stripy, printed pattern — will appeal to young people

Embroidered heart motif — will appeal to young people

Thick black cord — for strong handles

Metal eyelet — to prevent the fabric fraying or tearing

Front pocket — for small shopping purchases, mobile phone, or purse

EXAM TIP
When annotating design ideas in the exam make sure your notes explain how your idea fits the specification.

Evaluate Your Ideas Against the Design Specification

Have a good <u>think</u> about all your initial ideas and decide which is the <u>best</u> — i.e. the one that most <u>closely matches</u> the design specification. This should be your <u>final idea</u> that you go on to <u>develop</u>.

Now you need to present a <u>more detailed</u> version of your <u>final design idea</u>, including:

> <u>Sketches</u> — <u>more than one</u>, such as <u>front and back views</u> and sketches to show the <u>detail</u> of <u>specific parts</u> of your design.
>
> <u>Annotation</u> — <u>label</u> your design to show all the <u>design and construction details</u> (e.g. fastenings, colours, decoration, environmental issues) and <u>relate</u> everything back to the <u>specification</u>. Make sure you <u>explain</u> anything that's <u>unclear</u> on the sketches.

CAD is Computer-Aided Design

<u>Sketching</u> and <u>modifying</u> your design can be much <u>easier</u> and <u>quicker</u> on a <u>computer</u>.

1) <u>Computer-Aided Design</u> (CAD) involves <u>designing products</u> on a <u>computer</u>, rather than using the traditional method of sketching on paper.

2) CAD software includes <u>basic</u> drawing and painting software (e.g. Adobe® Illustrator®, CorelDRAW® and Adobe® Photoshop®) and more <u>specialised graphics software</u> (e.g. <u>Speed Step®</u> — which includes <u>ProSketch®</u> for <u>drawing</u> textile products and <u>ProPainter®</u> for adding <u>patterns/colours</u> and <u>3D modelling</u>).

3) Graphics software often contains <u>libraries</u> (<u>databases</u>) of lots of different <u>basic textile shapes</u> (e.g. sleeves etc.), which you can use to generate designs instead of drawing your own. Libraries may also include <u>textures</u> (e.g. woven, non-woven) and <u>colours</u> (e.g. those used by dye companies).

4) CAD can help you with <u>designing</u> and <u>developing</u> your ideas in many ways — see the next page.

Like a textiles X Factor — which idea gets to go to boot camp?

It might be tough to <u>reject</u> some of your ideas, but make sure you choose the one that <u>fits</u> the specification <u>best</u>, not just your favourite. It means you'll create a <u>better product</u> in the end.

Generating Design Ideas

CAD Can Help You Do The Following...

Produce MOOD BOARDS to help generate ideas, using stored or scanned images or photographs, patterns, text and music.

CAD is quicker than drawing by hand, and designs can be stored and reused without being redrawn.

PRODUCE DESIGN IDEAS using on-screen tools, images from the software's object library or by scanning in hand-drawn sketches. These ideas can then be stored on CDs or the hard drive so you can update them whenever you want.

DESIGN LOGOS, PRINTS and DECORATIVE PATTERNS, using different colours and textures from the software's library or from scanned images (e.g. digital camera photos). These designs can be used to produce 'virtual reality samples' of fabric or swatches (see below).

MODEL design ideas in 2D — you can try out different prints, patterns, colours and textures on your designs. You can also MODEL your ideas in 3D — design ideas can be simulated in 3D on photos or figurines and any necessary modifications made. A 3D simulation of your final design idea is called a 'virtual prototype'.

Create a SCALED WORKING DRAWING (see p.18) — the correct dimensions and measurements can be added to a drawing so it's to scale.

COMMUNICATE with the client/buyer — CAD images can be exported to email and sent to clients for approval, or presented as professional catalogue images.

See pages 44-45 for more on patterns and lay plans.

Create the PATTERN PIECES for your design and work out how to lay them out on the fabric (the 'lay plan') in a way that produces minimum waste. The CAD software automatically creates patterns in different sizes from the one design — this is called grading.

JAMES KING-HOLMES / SCIENCE PHOTO LIBRARY

- In schools, CAD software can be linked to CAM (computer-aided manufacture, see p.42) machines, which include dye-sublimation printers (that transfer ink to fabric using heat) and computerised sewing machines. You can use these machines to produce fabric swatches (samples), short runs of fabric to make a prototype, or embroidered logos.
- In industry, CAD software is linked to many different CAM machines, e.g. laser cutters.

Practice Questions

1) Rodney is doing a practice exam. These are his design ideas for an environmentally friendly, cool, summer shirt. Give four major things that are wrong with his design idea drawings.

2) Give two ways you could use CAD in the design process.

3) Give two advantages of using CAD to create pattern pieces.

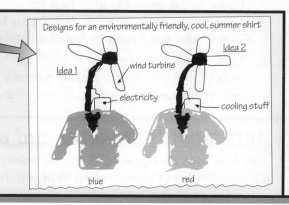

Designs for an environmentally friendly, cool, summer shirt

Idea 1

Idea 2

wind turbine

electricity

cooling stuff

blue

red

Design and Development

Now you've got your design idea you need to make sure it will fit the user...

Ergonomics Means Making the Product Fit the User

1) People come in all shapes and sizes, so most textiles products need to vary in size (e.g. clothes, sleeping bags) or be adjustable (e.g. rucksacks) to fit the user — this is known as ergonomics.

2) It can be important to design products ergonomically for health reasons, e.g. a badly-designed rucksack may damage your back if worn to carry heavy stuff repeatedly.

3) You also need to think about ergonomics when selecting fastenings. E.g. fiddly buttons are hard for little kids to do up — large toggles or Velcro® would be more ergonomic.

4) To design things ergonomically, you need to use anthropometric data...

> Anthropometrics is the collection of data on human body measurements. The data is gathered by taking detailed measurements of a wide range of body sizes. This data is then used to come up with measurements for standard clothes sizes (see below). Designers need to make products in these standard sizes so that they'll fit most people — this means the products will look good and be ergonomic.

Clothes are Usually made in Standard Sizes

1) Clothes use a variety of sizing methods depending on the age and sex of the consumer. They're all based on anthropometric data though.

- Anthropometric data shows that women's bust, waist and hips sizes are related. Women's clothes are produced in standard dress sizes based on these relative measurements. In the UK these are 6, 8, 10, 12 and so on.

- Children change size and shape quickly, so babies' clothes are sized in three month intervals up to 12 months and then in six month intervals up to 36 months. Children's clothes are often sized in one or two year intervals, e.g. 4-5 years (or sometimes they're sized by height).

- Men's shirts are often sized by collar size, and their trousers by waist size.

- Adult clothes, particularly trousers, come in different lengths to suit different heights of consumer. Some women's clothing ranges have petite styles for smaller women of up to about 5' 3".

2) Standard sizes mean people know what size they're likely to need when trying on and buying clothes. They also make clothes easier to be mass produced due to grading (see below).

3) But standard sizes only cater for about 90% of the population. People that don't fit into the standard range (e.g. very tall people) may have to go to a specialist clothing shop or have clothes made for them (bespoke clothing). A designer needs to think about whether their target market requires standard or specialist sizes.

Use Anthropometric Data When Designing Your Product

1) You need to use data on human body measurements to make sure your product fits a standard size.

2) If your target market is your own age group then it's a good idea to fit the prototype to yourself, but if your target market is 2 year olds, for example, you'll have to find the standard sizes for that age group.

It's important to remember to change the scale of details as well as the size of the garment.

3) You should make sure your product can be adapted to a range of different sizes. Making patterns for different sizes of the same garment is known as grading (see p.44).

Anthropoids are apes and arthropods are invertebrates...

...so take care with your spelling. The point is, you want your textile product to fit as many people as possible — it's not worth making stuff with really long arms if it'll only fit six people in the world.

Design and Development

When developing your final idea it's <u>not</u> just ergonomics and anthropometrics you need to bear in mind...

There's Lots to Consider When *Choosing Materials*

When <u>choosing fabrics</u> for your textiles products, you need to think about lots of <u>issues</u>
— there's more about this on pages 32-33. You need to think about the <u>same issues</u> when choosing <u>thread</u>, <u>fastenings</u>, <u>interfacing</u>, <u>elastic</u>, <u>sequins</u>, etc. for your textile product — these issues are:

- <u>Function</u> — choose components that will help the product <u>do what it's designed to do</u>, e.g. if the pocket on a bag needs to be secure, a zip might be better than a button.
- <u>Aesthetics</u> — choose components that will help the product <u>look good</u> and <u>appeal</u> to its <u>target market</u>, e.g. using thread that's the same colour as the fabric might look better on a garment.
- <u>Moral and cultural issues</u> — e.g. using elephant-ivory buttons would cause huge moral issues. And in China black is seen as bad luck, so if your product is going to be sold in China you won't want to choose black components (see p.57 for more on this sort of thing).
- <u>Costings</u> — make sure the <u>cost of the components</u> you choose is in keeping with the intended <u>cost of your product</u>, e.g. it's better to use cheap, synthetic buckles on a cheap bag, instead of silver ones. You might have to <u>modify</u> your design so it comes in at the <u>right budget</u>.
- <u>Environmental issues/sustainability</u> — think of any way in which you could <u>reduce</u> the <u>impact of your product</u> on the <u>environment</u>, e.g. you could reuse buttons from an old cardigan instead of new ones.

> You need to find a <u>compromise</u> between all these factors, e.g. using recycled components might affect the aesthetics too much, so you have to think about making the product more sustainable in a different way.

Creativity and *Sustainability* are *Important* in *Design*

Products that are <u>innovative</u> (<u>new</u>, <u>different</u>) and <u>sustainable</u> (have a <u>low impact</u> on the <u>environment</u>) will <u>appeal</u> to consumers and <u>sell</u> better than products that aren't. So make sure you <u>evaluate</u> your designs with this in mind:

> You could make your product <u>more innovative</u> by <u>changing</u> the <u>shape</u>, by <u>adding decoration</u>, by <u>combining fibres</u> (see p.26-27), by <u>adapting a current design</u> or by <u>filling a gap in the market</u>.

> You could make your product <u>more sustainable</u> by using fabrics and components that are <u>recyclable/recycled</u>, <u>reusable</u>, <u>biodegradable</u> or <u>organic</u>, by creating a <u>more economical lay plan</u> (see p.45), by using <u>non-toxic dyes</u>, or by <u>reducing</u> the amount of <u>energy used</u> in making it.

An innovative take on the classic evening dress.

There's more about sustainability on p.62-63.

Practice Questions

1) What is <u>ergonomics</u>? What <u>data</u> do you need to design something ergonomically?

2) Name the <u>sizing method</u> used for:
   a) women's clothing.
   b) babies' clothing.
   c) children's clothing.
   d) men's shirts.
   e) men's trousers.

3) Explain why you should consider <u>cost</u> issues when choosing materials for a textile product.

Development

I'm afraid there's more to development — now you need to <u>test</u> your design and make <u>improvements</u>.

You Should Test and Evaluate Your Design

1) You need to <u>test</u> your product design to see if it <u>does what you want it to do</u> — whether it fits the <u>design specification</u>. This is the <u>evaluation</u>. It's best to go through the design criteria one by one.

2) You'll probably find that parts of your design <u>don't work out</u> the way you wanted them to or don't fit the <u>design specification</u>. If so, you need to <u>think</u> about the <u>improvements</u> you could make. You need to be able to <u>reject</u> the part of the design that <u>doesn't work</u> and <u>justify</u> an <u>alternative</u>.

Design Specification for a Reusable Shopping Bag
- The finished bag must be retailed for £3 or less.
- It must be made out of environmentally-friendly material.
- It must be brightly-coloured.

E.g. maybe the reusable shopping bag <u>looks great</u> but the organic, stripy cotton is actually too <u>expensive</u>, so you could <u>reject</u> this fabric. Instead, you could find a <u>cheaper alternative</u> stripy, organic fabric, or you could use white organic cotton and <u>dye it yourself</u> — using a natural dye. Both of these ways mean the product still fits the specification.

1 By Modelling

Modelling is about <u>trying out</u> your design, so you can work out the finer <u>details</u> and <u>identify</u> problems.

1) You could start by doing more <u>detailed</u> drawings of your design to show the <u>construction</u> techniques (e.g. seams), <u>texture</u> of the fabric or the <u>exact design</u> of a <u>print</u>, <u>logo</u>, or <u>decoration</u> (e.g. beading).

2) Then try out the <u>decorative</u> or <u>construction</u> techniques on small <u>samples</u> of fabric.

3) You can model <u>different aspects</u> of your design (e.g. a sleeve, a pocket) to <u>experiment</u> with different shapes, fabrics and components.

using a zip... ... or using a popper...

E.g. model the pocket on the reusable shopping bag to test how different fastenings work with the fabric.

4) As you're modelling, you need to make the <u>paper pattern pieces</u> for your product — the <u>templates</u> you'll use for cutting out the fabric pieces. These will help you make a <u>prototype</u> (see below).

CAD (see p.13) can create 'virtual models and prototypes' you can see on-screen.

2 By Prototyping

1) After you've done some modelling you need to make a <u>prototype</u> — a <u>full-scale model</u> of your product. (In your controlled assessment this is the <u>first example</u> of your product.)

2) A prototype is made using the <u>pattern</u> and it allows you to <u>test out</u> the <u>correct size</u>, <u>shape</u>, <u>style</u>, <u>drape</u> etc. of your design — this means you can make any necessary <u>improvements</u> and <u>avoid wasting time and resources</u> on an imperfect product.

3) A prototype <u>doesn't</u> have to be made out of the <u>correct fabric</u> — in school, it might be made out of <u>paper</u> or <u>recycled fabric</u>, and in industry it's often made out of <u>calico</u> (cheap, white cotton). You could make <u>several</u> prototypes, using different materials, to find the best <u>aesthetics</u>.

4) In industry, prototypes can be used to test <u>manufacturing processes</u> so any potential <u>manufacturing problems</u> can be sorted out. They're also used to help <u>plan production</u> — e.g. by working out the amount of fabric/components needed, by planning the equipment and labour required, by calculating costings, etc.

Protoypes can also be used to check customer reactions (see next page).

Models — I knew there was a reason for doing GCSE textiles...

You're probably thinking that this development lark is a slow process, but it's a really important one. It means you can iron out all the problems with your design before you make it for real.

Development

3 By Considering Other People's Views

You could ask a <u>sample</u> of your <u>target market</u> to <u>try out</u> your <u>prototype</u>. Their <u>feedback</u> will help you <u>modify</u> your design so that it's <u>appealing</u> to the target market, is <u>fit for purpose</u> and will <u>sell</u> (hopefully).

E.g. young people might test the reusable shopping bag prototype and say that the cord handles make the empty bag bulky to carry around. This means you can <u>justify</u> making the straps out of cotton instead.

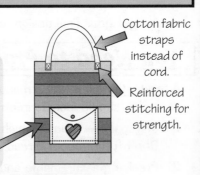

Cotton fabric straps instead of cord.

Reinforced stitching for strength.

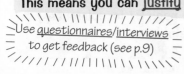

Use <u>questionnaires/interviews</u> to get feedback (see p.9)

You could also benefit from the experience of <u>experts</u> (professionals) in the textiles industry (e.g. designers, seamstresses, haberdashers, fabric store owners) by asking them to look at your design and <u>suggest improvements</u>.

Keep Going Until You Get it Just Right

You might find that you end up modifying something, then trying it out, then making <u>another</u> modification and trying that out, then making <u>another</u> modification and trying that out, and so on. That's just the way it goes sometimes.

Here's a summary of how it works <u>every time</u> you try something new:

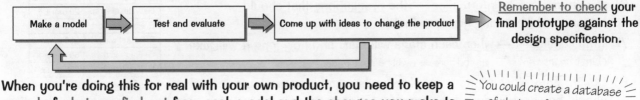

| Make a model | ➡ | Test and evaluate | ➡ | Come up with ideas to change the product |

➡ <u>Remember to check</u> your final prototype against the design specification.

When you're doing this for real with your own product, you need to keep a <u>record</u> of <u>what you find out</u> from each model and the <u>changes</u> you make to your design as a result.

You could create a database of photos of your models and the modifications.

Practice Questions

1) When you're <u>evaluating</u> your final design, <u>what</u> should you <u>check its features against</u>?

2) Suggest two reasons why you might make a <u>model</u> of part of your design.

3) What is a <u>prototype</u>?

4) Give <u>three</u> advantages of making a <u>prototype</u>.

5) You've made a <u>prototype</u> of a bag for <u>carrying snowboards</u>.
   a) Explain <u>why</u> it would be worthwhile getting some snowboarders to try it out.
   b) <u>Who else</u> might it help to show it to before you start final production, and why?

6) Tammy makes a <u>prototype</u> pyjama case in the shape of a dinosaur, with a button fastening for the mouth. When she asks her friends what they think about it, they say that the buttons don't look much like teeth. What could she do <u>next</u>?

Planning

You've got your final design, so you need to <u>plan</u> how you're going to make it.

You Need to Produce a Detailed Production Plan

A <u>production plan</u> tells a manufacturer exactly how to make a product — so it needs to be <u>detailed</u>. Your plan should include information on:

1) <u>Materials</u> — exactly which fabrics and pre-manufactured components are needed, including <u>amounts</u>. Don't forget about thread — you'll need to specify the colours of that too.

2) Precise <u>measurements</u> and <u>tolerances</u> for each part of your product (see page 67 for tolerances). And remember to include the <u>seam allowances</u>. A <u>working drawing</u> is useful here. This is a <u>detailed</u> drawing of the <u>finished product</u> with its <u>precise dimensions</u> in <u>millimetres</u>.

3) <u>Lay plans</u> for the <u>pattern pieces</u>. These should be as efficient as possible — for <u>cost</u> and <u>environmental</u> reasons.

4) The <u>tools and equipment</u> that are needed for each stage of the production process and how they'll be <u>used</u>. E.g. overlockers for finishing edges, needles for attaching beads.

5) <u>Processes</u> — what <u>construction techniques</u> will be used and what needs to be <u>prepared</u> before you can start each stage. For example, the fabric might need to be <u>ironed</u> before you mark out the pattern.

Remember — think about sustainability. It'll take less energy to heat up the iron once and iron lots, than to heat it up over and over to iron tiny amounts.

6) <u>Health and safety information</u> — the <u>precautions</u> that should be taken while making your product.

7) <u>Time schedules</u> — <u>when</u> each stage will start and <u>how long</u> it will take. Gantt charts are really useful here — see the next page.

8) <u>Quality control instructions</u> — where, when and how products should be <u>checked</u> during the manufacturing process.

Working drawing
— Reusable Shopping Bag

Front view   Back view

Garment details

A. Height of bag	400 mm ± 5
B. Width of bag	350 mm ± 5
C. Length of strap	500 mm ± 2
D. Width of strap	20 mm ± 1
E. Pocket height	150 mm ± 2
F. Pocket width	200 mm ± 2
G. Flap width	50 mm ± 1
H. Flap length	250 mm ± 1

Manufacturers Make Plans to Overcome Problems...

1) <u>Quality Assurance</u> (QA) procedures — e.g. servicing machinery regularly and checking materials as they come in — can help manufacturers avoid problems.

2) But no matter how good a plan is, problems can still arise during production — sometimes <u>machines break</u>, suppliers run out of <u>materials</u> or <u>components</u> and workers go <u>off sick</u>.

3) Manufacturers have to <u>plan</u> what they'll do if these things happen, e.g. have <u>spares</u> of commonly used machine parts (like needles), know <u>other suppliers</u> and <u>train</u> more than one person to do a job.

...You Might Need to Overcome Problems Too

For example, the shop might <u>run out</u> of the type of button you need — so you'll have to find another supplier, or use a different type of button.

Or you might realise that hand-sewing 12,000 individual sequins on will take approximately 5 years, and decide to use <u>sequined tape</u> instead.

In the <u>Controlled Assessment</u> you get marks for finding ways around tricky problems.

My final bag measures 6 by 8 by 4 mm... hum...

Here we are at the end of the design process... but don't rush this bit. The production plan needs to be detailed enough for someone to make your product <u>without ~~messing it up~~ messing it up</u>.

Planning

You need to plan your work to make the best use of <u>materials</u>, <u>equipment</u> and <u>time</u>.

Use Charts to Help You Plan Your Work

You need to work out <u>what order</u> to do things in.

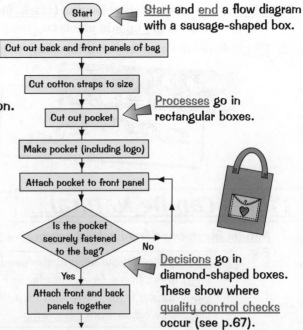

<u>Start</u> and <u>end</u> a flow diagram with a sausage-shaped box.

<u>Processes</u> go in rectangular boxes.

<u>Decisions</u> go in diamond-shaped boxes. These show where <u>quality control checks</u> occur (see p.67).

① **Work Order** This can be produced as a <u>table</u> or <u>flow chart</u>. The purpose of a work order is to plan the <u>sequence</u> of tasks to be carried out. The work order might include details of tools and equipment, quality control stages, safety, and so on. For example, for the resuable shopping bag:

Day	Process	Tools needed	
		School	Industry
1	Cut out back and front panels	Fabric scissors	Laser cutter
	Cut cotton straps to size	Fabric scissors	Laser cutter
	Cut out pocket	Fabric scissors	Laser cutter
2	Make pocket (including logo)	Embroidery machine & sewing machine	Embroidery machine & sewing machine

You also need to work out <u>how long</u> each stage will take, and how these times will fit into the <u>total time</u> you've allowed for production. One way to do this is with a Gantt chart:

② **Gantt Chart** The tasks are listed down the <u>left-hand</u> side, and the <u>timing</u> is plotted across the top. The coloured squares show <u>how long</u> each task takes, and the <u>order</u> they're done in.

Sometimes things overlap. E.g. if you'd screen printed a design on your bag, you could get on with making the handles while the ink dried.

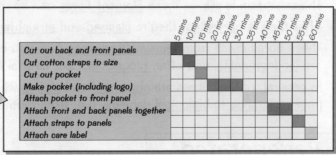

Test Products to Check They're Fit For Purpose

1) You need to <u>test</u> and <u>evaluate</u> your final product to see if it meets the <u>specification</u>.

2) For example, if the specification states that your bag must be <u>strong enough</u> to carry shopping in, put some tins of beans in it and carry it around for a bit. If you end up with a bruised toe, you need to <u>modify your design</u> and maybe use a stronger type of seam.

3) It's a good idea to get <u>other people's opinions</u> of the final product too.

Practice Questions

1) a) What is a <u>production plan</u>?
   b) What <u>information</u> should be included on a production plan?

2) What is the purpose of writing a <u>work order</u> chart?

3) Tim is planning the production of a T-shirt with a screen-printed design on it. What type of <u>chart</u> could he use that would show tasks that could be done while the ink from the screen-printed design is <u>drying</u>?

Types of Fibre

Now to the stars of the show — the fabrics. First up, the fibres and yarns that fabrics are made from.

Yarns Are Threads Made From Tiny "Hairs" Called Fibres

1) Fibres come in either short lengths (staple fibres), or longer lengths (filaments).
   Filaments can be cut up into staple lengths if required.

2) Staple fibres are spun (twisted together) to produce yarns. Filaments can be spun or used as they are.

Yarns made from filaments are smooth...

...while yarns made from staple fibres tend to be hairier.

Fibres Can Be Natural...

1) Natural fibres come from natural sources — plants and animals.
   E.g.

   - cotton fibres grow around the seed of the cotton plant
   - linen fibres come from the stem of the flax plant
   - wool comes from sheep and other animals
   - silk fibres come from silkworms

2) Natural fibres usually come in staple lengths
   (e.g. cotton fibres are a few centimetres long).
   The exception is silk — these filament fibres can be up to 1 km long.

3) After they're harvested, they're cleaned and straightened before being spun into a yarn.

4) These fibres come from renewable sources (i.e. you can always produce more of them), and the fibres
   are biodegradable, and often recyclable. So, natural fibres are fairly sustainable (see p.62-63).

5) In general, natural fibres are absorbent and strong when dry, but have
   poor resistance to biological damage, e.g. from moths and mildew (mould).

There's lots more on the properties of fibres and fabrics on pages 24–25.

...Regenerated...

1) Regenerated fibres are made from natural materials — usually cellulose from wood pulp.
   These materials are chemically treated to produce fibres.

2) Different fibres are made by using different chemicals.

   For example, viscose fibres are made by dissolving cellulose in sodium hydroxide solution.
   The liquid is forced through tiny holes, and hardened to form filament fibres. These filaments
   are stretched into a yarn which is wound onto spools, or chopped into staple lengths.

3) The fibres have a renewable origin, but many are made using synthetic chemicals,
   which makes them less sustainable than natural fibres. However, some regenerated
   fibres, like Tencel®, are produced so that almost all of the chemicals used can be
   recycled, and the fibres themselves are recyclable and biodegradable.

4) Regenerated fibres tend to have similar properties to natural fibres, but can be given
   different properties by using different chemicals. E.g. viscose can be made to drape well.

Rapunzel, Rapunzel — let down a yarn of many staple lengths...

Your clothes may not seem quite as glam once you know that they're made from chemically treated
wood pulp... But you still need to learn about where different fibres come from and how they're made.

Types of Fibre

...Or Manufactured

1) <u>Manufactured</u> or <u>synthetic fibres</u> are man-made.

2) They're made from <u>polymers</u> — <u>long chains</u> of <u>molecules</u>. These come mainly from <u>coal</u> or <u>oil</u>.

> E.g. <u>polyester</u>, <u>elastane</u> (better known as <u>LYCRA</u>®) and <u>acrylic</u> are produced from <u>oil</u>, and polyamide (<u>nylon</u>) is produced from <u>coal</u>.

Note: puppy not made of nylon.

3) The polymers are <u>melted</u> or <u>dissolved</u> in solution. This <u>liquid</u> is then forced through tiny <u>holes</u> and <u>hardened</u> to form <u>filament fibres</u>.

4) The <u>filaments</u> are <u>stretched</u> into a <u>yarn</u> which is <u>wound</u> onto spools, or <u>chopped</u> into <u>staple lengths</u>.

5) Because manufactured fibres are made from <u>non-renewable resources</u>, they're <u>less sustainable</u> than other types of fibre.

6) Synthetic fibres can be given many <u>different properties</u>. In general, they're <u>resistant</u> to <u>biological damage</u>, and can be <u>changed by heating</u>, e.g. to form permanent pleats and different textures. However, they're <u>not very absorbent</u>, so they can be hard to <u>dye</u>.

No matter what they threw at him, the new, synthetic James Bond just wouldn't dye.

Microfibres are Usually Manufactured Fibres

1) <u>Microfibres</u> are really <u>thin</u> fibres — they can be up to <u>100 times thinner</u> than human <u>hair</u>.

2) They're very <u>versatile</u> — they can be <u>woven</u>, <u>knitted</u>, or <u>bonded</u> to make fabrics (see p.22-23).

3) But they're <u>expensive</u>, so they're often <u>blended</u> with cotton, linen or silk to reduce costs (see p.26).

4) Microfibres can be woven so <u>tightly</u> that they stop water <u>droplets</u> from penetrating a fabric, but let water <u>vapour</u> (e.g. sweat) escape — this makes the fabric <u>water repellent</u> and <u>breathable</u>.

5) Microfibre-based <u>fabrics</u> are <u>soft</u>, <u>comfortable</u> to wear, <u>last well</u> and <u>hang</u> beautifully. Not to mention being <u>light weight</u> and <u>quick drying</u>. They're used to make underwear, sportswear, hosiery (e.g. tights), cleaning cloths and outdoor clothing.

6) These utterly brilliant fibres are also used for <u>micro-encapsulation</u> — just you wait until page 28.

Oh, go on then — take a quick peek now if you like.

Practice Questions

1) Fibres come as staple lengths or filaments. Which of the two is <u>longer</u>?

2) The picture to the right shows a close up of a section of yarn. Would you expect this yarn to have been made from <u>filaments</u> or <u>staple fibres</u>? <u>Explain</u> your answer.

3) Explain what makes <u>natural fibres</u> more <u>sustainable</u> than other types of fibre.

4) <u>Describe</u> how a <u>yarn of wool</u> is produced.

5) What are many <u>regenerated fibres</u> made from?

6) Give <u>two advantages</u> of using <u>manufactured fibres</u> over natural fibres.

7) Geoffrey is designing a pair of shorts. He wants the shorts to be <u>affordable</u>. Explain <u>why</u> Geoffrey <u>shouldn't</u> use a fabric made from 100% <u>microfibres</u>.

Fabric Construction

Fabrics are made from <u>yarns</u> (held together by weaving or knitting), or <u>fibres</u> (bonded or felted together).

Fabrics can be Made from *Woven Yarns...*

<u>Woven fabrics</u> are made by interlacing <u>two</u> sets of yarns — the <u>weft</u>, which travels from <u>right to left</u> (purple in the diagrams below), and the <u>warp</u>, which travels <u>up and down</u> the weave (green in the diagrams below). There are different weaves...

PLAIN WEAVE

1) The simplest weave — the weft yarn passes over and under <u>alternate</u> warp yarns, making it <u>unpatterned</u>.

2) It's <u>hardwearing</u> — <u>strong</u> and holds its <u>shape</u> well. It has a <u>smooth</u> finish (making it good for printing on).

3) It's the <u>cheapest</u> weave to produce and is used to make loads of fabrics, especially <u>cotton-based</u> ones.

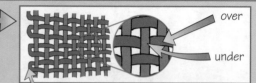

over
under

The <u>edge</u> of a woven piece of fabric, where the weft yarns wrap around the warp yarns, is called the <u>selvedge</u>.

TWILL WEAVE

1) A twill weave creates a <u>diagonal pattern</u> on the surface of the fabric. E.g. the weft yarn goes <u>over two</u> yarns and <u>under one</u>. The next weft yarn repeats this, but one warp yarn further along.

2) It's <u>stronger</u> and <u>drapes better</u> than plain weave. It's used for fabrics such as <u>denim</u>.

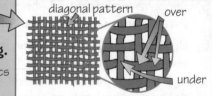

diagonal pattern over

under

SATIN WEAVE

1) The weft yarn goes <u>over four or more</u> warp threads and <u>under one</u>.

2) The long weft yarns on the surface (called <u>floats</u>) catch the light, so satin weave makes <u>shiny</u> fabrics (like <u>satin</u>).

3) But the floats can <u>snag</u>, so the fabric is quite <u>delicate</u> and <u>doesn't resist abrasion</u> (wear caused by rubbing).

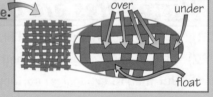

over under

float

JACQUARD WEAVE

1) Jacquard weaving uses an <u>automated system</u> to control each <u>warp</u> thread <u>individually</u> — so, for <u>each row</u> of the weave, you can decide which warp threads the weft will go <u>over</u> and which it will go <u>under</u>.

2) This lets you weave very <u>complicated</u> patterns.

3) It's a relatively <u>expensive</u> process, though, so it's only used for specialist fabrics like <u>damask</u>.

CUT PILE and LOOPED FABRICS

1) These fabrics are made using an <u>extra set</u> of threads (<u>pile threads</u>). <u>Warp pile</u> fabrics (e.g. velvet) have two sets of warp threads. <u>Weft pile</u> fabrics (e.g. corduroy) have two sets of weft threads.

2) The pile threads are woven over <u>metal rods</u>, so they stand out in <u>loops</u> from the 'ground' weave. These loops can be cut to form a <u>cut pile fabric</u>.

3) Cut pile fabrics have a <u>soft</u> surface finish, but don't tend to be hard-wearing. They're easily <u>crushed</u> and tend to <u>shed</u> the pile.

4) These fabrics are <u>directional</u>, so pattern lay plans must be <u>carefully designed</u> and there's likely to be quite a bit of fabric <u>wasted</u>.

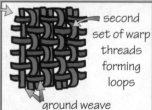

second set of warp threads forming loops

ground weave

Aren't fabwics twilling — we'd be beweft without them...

It's easy to know <u>warp</u> from <u>weft</u>, 'cos <u>weft</u> goes from <u>weft</u> to <u>right</u> (tee hee). The rest needs some careful learning, but with practice you'll soon be able to spot a twill weave at 50 metres...

Fabric Construction

...Knitted Yarns...

Knitted fabrics are made by interlocking one or more yarns together using loops.
These loops trap air, making knitted fabrics good insulators. They also stretch more than woven fabrics.
There are a couple of types you need to know about:

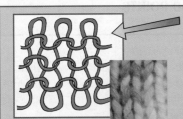

Weft-knitted fabrics — can be produced by hand or machine

1) The yarn runs across the fabric, making interlocking loops with the row of yarn beneath.
2) These fabrics stretch and can lose their shape easily.
3) If the yarn breaks it can unravel and make a 'ladder'.
4) They're used for jumpers, socks and T-shirts.

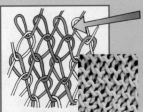

Warp-knitted fabrics — can only be produced by machines (which can be expensive).

1) The yarns run "up" the fabric, in loops, which interlock vertically.
2) They're stretchy but still keep their shape.
3) These fabrics are hard to unravel and are less likely to ladder.
4) Tights, swimwear, fleeces, and some bed sheets are all made from warp-knitted fabrics.

...or Non-woven Fibres

Non-woven fabrics are layers of fibres held together by bonding or felting.
They don't fray, and can be cut in any direction — which means there's little waste when laying out patterns. However, they don't stretch and aren't very strong.

BONDED FABRICS

1) These are "webs" of fibres held together by glue, stitches, needle-punching or heat.

Stitch-bonded non-woven fabric
fibres
stitching

2) They're used for interfacing (see p.39), artificial leather and disposable cloths (e.g. medical masks).

FELTED FABRICS

1) Felting is an older way of making non-woven fabric.
2) Wool felt is made by combining pressure, moisture and heat to interlock a mat of wool fibres.
3) Needle felts are made using a felting needle. This is a straight needle with barbs along its length. When you push the needle into loose fibres, the barbs pull the fibres together to make felt.
4) Felt is used for carpet underlay, craft material, hats, jewellery and snooker table coverings.

Practice Questions

1) When you're making a woven fabric, in which direction does:
   a) the weft yarn travel?
   b) the warp yarn travel?

2) State the type of weave which:
   a) creates a diagonal pattern on the surface of the fabric.
   b) can create very complicated patterns.
   c) has long weft yarns on the surface called floats.
   d) is the cheapest to produce.

3) Give three disadvantages of cut pile fabrics.

4) Keen bird watcher Egbert wants to design some trousers that stretch but don't lose their shape. Should Egbert use weft-knitted or warp-knitted fabric?

Section Two — Materials and Components

Fibres and Fabrics

Now to the <u>properties</u> of fabrics made from <u>natural</u> and <u>regenerated</u> fibres.

	FIBRE	USED IN THESE FABRICS	CHARACTERISTICS IN FABRICS		USES
			GOOD POINTS	**BAD POINTS**	
NATURAL FIBRES	<u>COTTON</u> (from seed pods of cotton plant — fairly cheap)	E.g. denim, corduroy, calico	Resistant to abrasion, strong even when wet, absorbent, cool (high thermal conductivity), can be washed at high temperatures, alkali resistant, bleach-safe.	Poor elasticity, can shrink when washed, dries slowly, creases easily, high flammability, usually dissolved by acids, highly susceptible to moth and mildew damage.	Jeans, T-shirts, blouses, soft furnishings.
	<u>WOOL</u> (from sheep's fleece — fairly expensive)	E.g. knitted fabrics, Harris Tweed, gabardine, jersey, felt	Quite strong (strength depends on fibres used), good elasticity, very absorbent, warm (an insulator), crease-resistant, very low flammability.	Pilling (balls of fibres on the surface) occurs with abrasion, shrinks if washed at high temperatures, dries slowly, dissolved by acids, alkalis and chlorine bleach, susceptible to moth and mildew damage.	Suits, jumpers, coats, dresses, carpets.
	<u>LINEN</u> (from stalks of flax plant — can be expensive)	Linen	Resistant to abrasion, strong even when wet, absorbent, very cool (very high thermal conductivity), can be washed at high temperatures, alkali resistant, bleach-safe, moth resistant.	Poor elasticity, creases badly, high flammability, dissolved by acids, susceptible to mildew damage.	Trousers, summer suits, dresses, furnishings.
	<u>SILK</u> (from silkworm cocoons — expensive)	E.g. organza, chiffon, satin	Moderate abrasion resistance, very strong, absorbent, quite warm (low thermal conductivity), low flammability, moderate resistance to acids and alkalis.	Weaker when wet, quite poor elasticity, creases easily, might not wash well (usually needs to be dry cleaned), dissolved by chlorine bleach, susceptible to moth and mildew damage.	Lingerie, underwear, dresses, shirts, ties.
REGENERATED FIBRES	<u>VISCOSE</u> (from wood pulp treated with sodium hydroxide — fairly cheap)	E.g. rayon	Absorbent, cool (high thermal conductivity), moderate abrasion resistance, easily washable, moderate resistance to acids and alkalis, bleach-safe, moth resistant.	Weak when wet, poor elasticity, high flammability, highly susceptible to mildew damage.	Lingerie, underwear, dresses, suits, linings, soft furnishings.
	<u>ACETATE</u> (from wood pulp treated with acetic acid — fairly cheap)		Absorbent, dries quickly, cool (high thermal conductivity), resistant to moth and mildew damage.	Poor abrasion resistance, weak (particularly when wet), poor elasticity, dry cleaning recommended, high flammability, dissolved by acids and alkalis.	Linings, soft furnishings.

<u>Why does it always rayon me — this Harris Tweed dries slowly...</u>

You'll need to <u>justify</u> your fabric <u>selections</u> in your designs, so learn these properties. Next synthetics...

Fibres and Fabrics

Next, properties of fabrics made from synthetic fibres...

FIBRE	USED IN THESE FABRICS	CHARACTERISTICS IN FABRICS		USES
		GOOD POINTS	BAD POINTS	
POLYESTER (produced from oil — cheap)	E.g. dacron	Resistant to abrasion, strong (even when wet), good elasticity, easily washable, dries very quickly, crease resistant, holds heat-set pleats, low flammability, resists most chemical damage, moth and mildew resistant.	Not absorbent, dissolved by strong acids, thermoplastic so care needed when ironing (fibres will melt above a certain temperature).	Sportswear, bed sheets, curtains, cushions, padding, table cloths.
ELASTANE (produced from oil — fairly cheap)	E.g. LYCRA®	Resistant to abrasion, strong, extremely elastic (stretches up to 7 times its length), easily washable, resists most chemical damage, moth and mildew resistant.	Not absorbent, high flammability, dissolved by chlorine bleach.	Sports/swim wear, underwear, combined with other fibres to add stretch.
POLYAMIDE (produced from coal — fairly cheap)	E.g. nylon	Resistant to abrasion, very strong, good elasticity, warm (an insulator), easily washable, holds heat-set pleats, resists most chemical damage, moth and mildew resistant.	Not very absorbent, thermoplastic so care needed when ironing, melts as it burns.	Sportswear, furnishings, carpets, tights, socks.
ACRYLIC (produced from oil — cheap)		Strong when dry, good elasticity, quite warm (low thermal conductivity), doesn't shrink, resists most chemical damage, moth and mildew resistant.	Pilling can occur with abrasion, weak when wet, not very absorbent, high flammability.	Fake fur, knitted clothes, furnishings.

Practice Questions

1) State the fibre used to make these fabrics:
    a) denim   b) gabardine   c) chiffon

2) Give two positive and two negative properties of a fabric made from:
    a) 100% cotton   b) 100% wool

3) State one positive and one negative property of elastane.

4) Suggest why polyester is often used to make pyjamas.

5) A polyester shirt and a cotton shirt are stored in a damp cellar. Which would you expect to be in better condition after one month? Explain your answer.

6) Henry wants a fabric that feels cool in warm weather to use for a pair of summer trousers.
    a) Suggest a suitable fabric that Henry could use.
    b) Identify one drawback in using this fabric.

7) Steve has just completed his design for a pair of boxer shorts made from Harris Tweed. Give a reason why this is not an appropriate fabric to use for boxer shorts and suggest a more suitable alternative.

Fabric Combinations

You might think you know the <u>properties</u> of every type of <u>fibre</u> by now, but you're not finished yet. Don't worry though, these aren't <u>new types</u> of fibre — you're just learning about <u>mixing fibres together</u>.

Useful Fabrics Can Be Made by Combining Fibres

A fabric made from <u>one type of fibre</u> (e.g. 100% cotton) mightn't have <u>all the properties</u> you want for your product. Fabrics made from a <u>combination of different fibres</u> can give you <u>better</u> characteristics. But, <u>watch out</u> — you can also get some <u>less desirable</u> characteristics mixed in.

There are <u>several reasons</u> why you might want to combine fibres, such as:

1 APPEARANCE
You can create interesting <u>colour effects</u>, e.g. by using fibres with different levels of <u>absorbency</u> — the fibres take up different amounts of dye, creating different tones. You can also create interesting <u>textures</u>, e.g. by using some smooth fibres and some which are rougher.

2 PRACTICAL QUALITIES
You could make your fabric <u>more hard-wearing</u> by including <u>more durable fibres</u>. Or you could make a fabric <u>more crease resistant</u>, by adding <u>synthetic fibres</u>.

3 WORKING QUALITIES
You could get your fabric to <u>drape</u> better, or to keep its <u>shape</u>, by including fibres that have those properties.

4 COSTS
Combining an <u>expensive</u> fibre (e.g. silk) with a <u>cheaper one</u> (e.g. cotton), often means you can keep many of the <u>characteristics</u> of the <u>expensive</u> fibre but in a <u>cheaper</u> fabric — making your product easier to sell.

Fibres Can Be Combined by Blending...

1) A <u>blend</u> is when two or more <u>different fibres</u> are combined to produce a <u>yarn</u>.
2) These fibres are blended before or during <u>spinning</u>.
3) This mixed yarn is then <u>woven</u> or <u>knitted</u> to make a fabric.

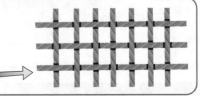

EXAMPLE — BLENDING COTTON AND POLYESTER FIBRES GIVES A REALLY USEFUL FABRIC

Cotton	Polyester
Hard-wearing & strong	Hard-wearing & very strong
Absorbent	Not absorbent
Dries slowly	Dries quickly
Creases easily	Doesn't crease
Shrinks easily	Doesn't shrink
Highly flammable	Not very flammable

Using a <u>blend</u> of polyester and cotton fibres you can create a fabric that:
- is even <u>stronger</u> and remains <u>hard-wearing</u>
- is <u>less absorbent</u> — so dries more quickly
- resists <u>creasing</u> (is easier to iron)
- <u>doesn't shrink</u> easily
- but is <u>highly flammable</u> ⇐ Watch out for <u>negative</u> properties.

Other examples include blending wool with <u>nylon</u> to make more <u>hard-wearing</u> carpets, and blending <u>silk</u> with <u>polyester</u> to make fabric that has the <u>qualities</u> of <u>silk</u>, but is <u>cheaper</u> and <u>easier</u> to care for.

Combined fibres — not like putting prunes on your bran flakes...

...I prefer to blend up a smoothie for breakfast anyway. Make sure you <u>learn</u> the advantages of combining fibres and the <u>two different ways</u> that you can do it — by <u>blending</u> and <u>mixing</u>...

Fabric Combinations

...or Mixing

1) A mix is when a fabric is made up of two or more different types of yarn.
2) For example, you could weave a fabric using one type of yarn for the warp and another for the weft.

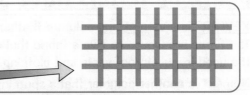

EXAMPLE — ELASTANE MIXED WITH COTTON MAKES A STRETCHIER FABRIC

Cotton	Elastane (LYCRA®)
Absorbent	Not absorbent
Not stretchy	Stretchy
Strong	Crease resistant

By mixing elastane and cotton yarns you can create a fabric that:
- is strong
- stretches to fit snugly
- resists creasing
- can be dyed easily

EXAM TIP:
Make sure you give specific examples of how the properties change when you combine fibres. Don't just say it's "durable".

Cotton-elastane mixtures are often used for swimwear and tight-fit jeans.

You can also mix different yarns to create decorative effects — e.g. different colours of silk can be mixed to create two-tone taffeta, or metallic yarns can be mixed in to create glittery fabrics.
Ripstop fabrics can be made by weaving thick nylon fibres into cotton, silk or polyester to add strength.

Fabrics Can Be Made by Coating or Laminating

COATING IS WHEN A LAYER OF POLYMER FILM IS APPLIED TO THE SURFACE OF A FABRIC

Coating a fabric with a polymer such as Teflon® or PVC makes it stain resistant and waterproof.
PVC coatings are often given to cotton or viscose to make protective garments for industry, or wipe clean tablecloths.

LAMINATED FABRICS ARE MADE FROM DIFFERENT LAYERS OF FABRIC STUCK TOGETHER

Lamination can be used with delicate fabrics — to add strength from an under layer, or protection from an outer layer. It can also add useful properties, e.g. a layer of foam could be used to make a fabric more insulating. GORE-TEX® and SympaTex® products are examples of laminated fabrics (see next page).

Practice Questions

1) Give four reasons why you might combine fibres to make a fabric.
2) Which fibre would you use to make a fabric more crease resistant — cotton or elastane?
3) Describe the two ways of combining fibres in fabrics.
4) Give three advantages of using a blend of cotton and polyester to make a fabric, rather than just cotton.
5) Why might you want to apply a PVC coating to a fabric?
6) How are laminated fabrics made?

Smart and Modern Materials

Now for some really, really clever fibres and fabrics.

Modern Materials Have Some Really Useful Properties

1) KEVLAR® is a very strong polymer that's made chemically and can be spun into strong fibres. The fibres are woven to give a fabric that's really, really strong and resistant to abrasion. It's used in bulletproof vests and clothing for motorcyclists.

2) Nomex® is another polymer that's spun into fibres. It's very fire-resistant and is used in firefighters' clothing and racing drivers' overalls.

3) Elastanes like LYCRA® are very elastic polymer fibres. They can be mixed with other fibres to make stretchy fabrics (see previous page). LYCRA® is used in hosiery (e.g. tights) and sportswear.

4) Neoprene is a strong, lightweight, synthetic rubber that's used to make wetsuits.

5) Polartec® fleece is a soft polyester velour used for outdoor clothing. It's insulating, quick-drying, breathable and very lightweight.

Velour is a knitted, stretchy fabric that feels like velvet.

Some Fabrics are Breathable

GORE-TEX® and SympaTex® fabrics are laminated fabrics — see previous page.

A GORE-TEX® membrane contains lots of tiny pores which allow water vapour (i.e. perspiration) to escape, but are too small for bigger rain droplets to pass through — it's both waterproof and breathable. A GORE-TEX® product is made by laminating a GORE-TEX® membrane between an outer and an inner layer of fabric. This makes the product sturdier. This material is used in loads of outdoor clothing.

A SympaTex® membrane is a mix of two different polymers — a waterproof polyester and a water vapour permeable polyether. The polyether lets water vapour escape, while the polyester keeps rain out. SympaTex® products are laminated in a similar way to GORE-TEX® ones.

Micro-encapsulation Lets You Put Chemicals in Fabrics

1) Micro-encapsulation is where a tiny droplet of chemical is coated in a shell — called a micro-capsule.

2) These micro-capsules can be embedded in microfibre fabrics (see p.21), to give the fabric different properties. As the garment is worn, the micro-capsules gradually burst and the chemicals are released.

3) Chemicals like perfumes, insect repellents, vitamins and odour neutralisers can all be embedded in fabrics using this method.

4) Examples of products that use this technology are antibacterial socks and scented lingerie.

Some Textiles Include Electronics

Conductive fabrics are starting to be used to integrate electronic microchips into textile products. They conduct electricity through a conductive network of fibres, while still being comfortable to wear. Conductive fabrics can supply power to a range of components. Applications include:

- Sensors in clothes that monitor heart rate and blood pressure.
- Washable electronic switches integrated into clothing to operate things like MP3 players and mobile phones.
- Fabric that acts as an electrical heater — used in things like car seats and motorbike clothing.

Conductive fabrics are 'smart' if they react automatically to different conditions — see next page.

Lamb-ination — so that's how sheep keep the rain out...

There are loads of clever things you can do with textiles. I've made a special camping suit — it keeps rain and midges out, stops you sweating, feeds you breakfast and keeps you smelling good at all times.

Smart and Modern Materials

Smart Materials _React to_ Environmental Conditions

1) Smart materials react automatically to changes in their surroundings, e.g. light, temperature or pressure.

2) Some smart materials can be produced using micro-encapsulation (see previous page), but these don't tend to withstand washing very well.

3) Intelligent polymer systems are being developed to get around this problem. These fabrics are woven from polymer fibres that are sensitive to heat, light, pressure, etc., so they don't need added chemicals to make them work. They're being used to develop military and medical applications.

> **Thermochromic fabric**
> 1) Micro-encapsulated dye changes colour at different temperatures.
> 2) The colour changing effect is lost after 5-10 washes because the micro-capsules burst.

4) In textiles, 'smart' is also used to refer more generally to 'functional' fabrics with special properties:

Anti-stress or calm-inducing fabrics — these fabrics are micro-encapsulated with aromatherapy oils.

Wrinkle-free fabrics — traditional fibres, like cotton, are coated with nanoparticles (particles or fibres a few millionths of a millimetre across). These particles stop the fabric from creasing without affecting its texture (see next page for more on nanoparticles).

Heat-generating fibres — these fibres heat up as they absorb moisture (an exothermic reaction, if you want to get technical). They're used in the linings of some top-of-the-range cold-weather jackets.

Anti-allergy fabrics — used in bedding, these are very tightly-woven fabrics that form a barrier against dust mites living in mattresses, pillows and duvets.

Sanitised or anti-fungal fabrics — these fabrics contain anti-bacterial or anti-fungal chemicals (often both) to prevent damage, stains, smells and health problems caused by microbes. Modern anti-microbial fabrics tend to be embedded with silver nanoparticles.

Moisture management systems — these are fabrics that actively draw moisture away from the skin (called 'wicking') and let it escape from the fabric. They're used a lot in sports clothing.

New _Materials are Being_ Developed _All the Time_

1) Lots of money and effort is being spent at the moment, trying to develop better and 'smarter' fabrics.

2) One smart fabric that's been in development for years is smart skin.

> This is a flexible material, like ordinary fabric, embedded with an array of tiny sensors. The sensors can detect tiny changes in temperature, moisture levels, electrical activity, etc. in your body, and they also detect chemicals in the air. The sensors then send the information to a monitor. The developers hope to use smart skin to make sensitive baby monitoring equipment.

Practice Questions

1) What modern fabric would be most useful for:
   a) overalls for a racing car refueller?
   b) clothing for a wind-surfer?
   c) knee-pad covers for a skateboarder?

2) Suggest three applications for micro-encapsulation.

3) Explain what is meant by a smart fabric.

4) Describe how a fabric can be made so that it is crease resistant.

5) Stacy is designing a jacket for mountain-climbers. Suggest two 'smart' or 'functional' fabrics that she might want to include in her design. Explain your answer.

Nanotechnology

Nanotechnology sounds like the sort of stuff that'd feature in an eighties time-travel film where they go all the way forward to the year 2010. So I reckon it's time to put on your all-in-one silver lamé suit...

Nanotechnology Deals with Things on a Tiny Scale

1) Nanoparticles are really really really really tiny bits of material — so tiny that you could fit about a thousand of them into the width of one of the hairs on this dog.

Dog

2) Nanoparticles of a substance often have different properties from the normal substance. This means materials made from (or containing) nanoparticles may have very different properties from normal materials.

Fabrics can be Coated with Nanoparticles

Fibres and fabrics can be given all kinds of great properties by coating them with a layer of nanoparticles:

1) Stain-repellent coating — this prevents dirt and oil sticking to the fibres in a fabric and stops the fibres from absorbing moisture. This makes fabrics much easier to clean — spillages and dirt can just be wiped off. Fabrics with this coating can still be machine washed and dry-cleaned.

Normal surface

Blue juice sticks easily to favourite yellow shirt and soaks in. Boo.

Nanoparticle coated

Juice drops make beads and roll off the smooth surface. Hooray.

2) Chemical-resistant coating — this reacts with any chemicals spilled onto the fabric and makes them safe so that the wearer isn't harmed. Fabrics with this coating could be used in the military or to make protective clothing for the chemical industry.

3) Fire-resistant coating — this is made out of 'clay' nanoparticles that are heat resistant, so they protect the fabric and the wearer from fire. Fabrics with this coating could be used to make protective clothing for the fire service.

The main advantage of using nanoparticle coatings over 'standard' finishes (see p.36-37) is that they don't change the feel of the fabric, so the wearability of the fabric isn't affected.

Nanotubes Conduct Heat and Electrical Signals

Nano-men hard at work making nanotubes.

1) Carbon nanotubes are really thin tubes of carbon — they're about one millionth of a millimetre in diameter.

2) Nanotubes conduct heat and electrical signals, and can be incorporated into fabrics.

3) For example, fabrics made using nanotubes could contain electrical sensors that monitor body temperature and heart rate (e.g. smart skin — see p.29).

4) The nanotubes don't add any weight or bulk to fabric, so they can be integrated into a fabric without affecting its wearability.

5) Unfortunately, nanotubes are really expensive to produce.

My Nan couldn't even work the DVD player...

Wow, this is all pretty crazy stuff to get your head round — make sure you take the time to really understand it though, 'cause examiners love asking questions about these really up-to-date things.

Nanotechnology

Nanothreads Can Promote Healing

1) <u>Nanothreads</u> are very very thin <u>fibres</u>.
2) Scientists have made nanothreads from <u>proteins</u> found in human <u>blood</u> that promote <u>blood clotting</u>.
3) These nanothreads have been made into <u>mesh pads</u>. When used on wounds they <u>encourage</u> the <u>blood to clot</u> quickly and so promote <u>healing</u>.
4) These mesh pads could be used to <u>stop bleeding</u> during <u>surgery</u> or on the <u>battlefield</u>.

If only they'd had nanothreads in my day...

Biotechnology Makes Use of Living Organisms

1) Scientists have created <u>genetically modified</u> goats to produce <u>milk</u> containing <u>proteins</u> from <u>spider's silk</u>.
2) The milk is <u>harvested</u> and <u>purified</u>, and the proteins are extracted and <u>spun into fibres</u>.
3) The material made from these fibres is called <u>BioSteel</u>®.
4) <u>BioSteel</u>® has the properties of <u>spider's silk</u> — it's <u>incredibly strong</u>, <u>lightweight</u> and <u>flexible</u>.
5) It's possible that BioSteel® could be used for making things like <u>bulletproof vests</u> and <u>medical stitches</u>.

A genetically modified organism is an organism that's had its DNA altered.

1) '<u>Victimless leather</u>' is an attempt to make <u>leather</u> in the <u>laboratory</u>, using <u>cells</u> from <u>living organisms</u>.
2) This <u>artificial leather</u> could be used in place of natural leather that's made from <u>dead animals</u>.
3) Some scientists have <u>grown animal tissue</u> in the <u>shape</u> of a <u>jacket</u> to demonstrate how this technology could be used in the future.

Practice Questions

1) What is a <u>nanoparticle</u>?
2) a) Describe how coating a fabric with nanoparticles can make it <u>stain resistant</u>.
   b) What <u>two</u> other <u>properties</u> could a fabric coated with nanoparticles have?
3) What is the <u>advantage</u> of nanoparticle coatings compared to 'standard' fabric finishes?
4) What are <u>nanotubes</u>?
5) Give <u>two properties</u> of nanotubes.
6) How do dressings made from nanothreads <u>promote healing</u>?
7) Give <u>two reasons</u> why BioSteel® could be a good material to use for bulletproof clothing.

Choosing Fabrics

Unless you're making the emperor's new clothes, you'll to need to choose a fabric for your product...

Pick Your Fabric Carefully

How fit for purpose your textile product is depends on whether you've chosen an appropriate fabric. Fabrics all have different properties. These properties can be divided into two categories:

- Physical (functional) properties
- Aesthetic properties

The properties of a fabric are influenced by the fibres that it's made from (see p.24-25) and also the construction technique used to make the fabric, e.g. the weave (see p.22-23).

Choose a Fabric Based on its Physical Properties...

Durability

1) Many clothes need to be strong and resistant to abrasion, e.g. children's wear and outdoor clothes.
2) If you need strong, hard-wearing fibres choose something like cotton, polyester or nylon.
3) Use a plain or twill weave fabric such as denim for strength.
4) Some synthetic fabrics, such as woven KEVLAR®, are very, very strong and resistant to abrasion.

Thermal Conductivity

1) Many clothes are designed to keep the wearer warm (e.g. a climbing jacket), others are designed to keep the wearer cool (e.g. a running vest).
2) For fabrics to keep you warm, use fibres that have low thermal conductivity (i.e. good insulators of heat), e.g. wool or acrylic.
3) Knitted fabrics are good insulators — air trapped in the loops keeps you warm.
4) Fine fibres loosely woven into a fabric will have high thermal conductivity, allowing heat to escape. Linen and fabrics made from acetate have high thermal conductivity.

Comfort

1) Everyday clothes should be comfortable to wear.
2) This might mean using fibres that are:
   Absorbent — natural and regenerated fibres wick moisture away from the skin.
   Stretchy — you can mix in synthetic fibres (e.g. elastane) to add elasticity.
3) Warp-knitted fabrics are comfortable — they will stretch but keep their shape.

Washability

1) Some products will need washing regularly, e.g. children's clothing.
2) Use machine-washable fibres (cotton can be washed at high temperatures) and fibres that dry quickly and resist creasing, e.g. polyester.
3) A plain woven fabric will be strong and unlikely to shrink, but knitted fabrics will resist creasing.

Flammability

1) Certain textile products, e.g. upholstery, need to be fire resistant by law.
2) It's important for some garments to have low flammability, e.g. nightclothes. 100% polyester is a suitable fabric.
3) Some things should be made from a flame proof fabric such as Nomex®, e.g. fire-fighters' clothing.

Thermal conductivity — a shock in your winter pants...

It must have been easier back in caveman times — "well you've got fur, or leaves... leaves have good stain resistance but aren't comfy or durable, so we'll use fur — it's soft, warm, and very 6752 BC."

Choosing Fabrics

I couldn't quite squeeze all the physical properties onto one page I'm afraid — there's just one more to go.

Resistance

1) Many fabrics can be damaged by coming into contact with different substances or organisms.
2) You may need to choose fabrics that are resistant to:

Acids and alkalis — use synthetic fibres as these are generally more resistant than natural ones.

Bleach — plant-based fibres such as cotton or linen or synthetic fibres like polyamide and acrylic.

Moths and mildew — all synthetic fibres are resistant as moths and mildew feed on natural fibres.

...and its Aesthetic Properties

A fabric's aesthetic properties describe its appearance. People might not know how well a textile product will perform when they first see it — but the fabric's aesthetic properties are likely to be the first thing to catch their eye. Colour and texture are obviously important qualities, but you also need to consider:

Drape

1) This is how well the fabric hangs or falls.
2) A good drape is important for garments like evening dresses.
3) Silk and viscose drape well — KEVLAR®, not so well.

Lustre

1) This is how well a fabric reflects light — a fabric with a good lustre will look glossy rather than dull.
2) Fibres such as silk and viscose have a good lustre.
3) Fabrics made using a satin weave also have a good lustre, as the long weft yarns catch the light.

There are also Other Issues to Consider

As well as the physical and aesthetic properties, you may need to consider the following issues when selecting a suitable fabric for a product:

1) Cost — certain fabrics are very expensive, so you may need to choose a cheaper alternative. E.g. silk is very expensive, but viscose has many of the same properties and is much cheaper.

2) Cultural — different cultures have different views on exposing flesh, so you would need to consider these views, e.g. by not selecting transparent fabrics to make clothes.

3) Ethical — you may wish to choose fabrics that have been ethically traded, which means that producers have been paid fairly for their products. You should also consider whether people will object to wearing clothes made from animal fur or leather, and consider using synthetic alternatives.

4) Environmental sustainability — natural fibres are more sustainable than synthetic fibres because they come from renewable sources. Organically farmed natural fibres have an even less harmful effect on the environment as they are grown without using certain man-made chemicals and pesticides.

Practice Questions

1) Charlotte is making a sail for a toy yacht. The sail will often be damp.
   a) Suggest two properties the fabric she chooses for the sail should have.
   b) Suggest what type of weave would be most suitable for the sail.

2) Suggest a type of fabric that would be suitable for each of the following. Explain your choice.
   a) bathroom curtains
   b) a cleaner's overalls
   c) promotional T-shirts for an environmental group

3) Maggie is making the costumes for a pantomime.
   She decides to make Cinderella's dress from viscose.
   a) Explain why this is a good choice.
   b) Maggie considered using silk at first. Suggest why Maggie decided against silk.

Dyeing and Printing

Thank goodness for <u>dyeing</u> and <u>printing</u> — otherwise we'd all be wearing slightly <u>off-white</u> clothes...

Dyeing Adds Colour to All of a Fabric

Dyeing can be done on a small scale by hand, (see pages 52-53) or in huge amounts <u>commercially</u>. In commercial dyeing, the fabric is dyed a <u>uniform colour</u>. It can be done in <u>batches</u> or <u>continuously</u>...

Batch Dyeing

1) In <u>batch dyeing</u>, a <u>batch</u> of fabric (a specific amount) is dyed with <u>one colour</u>, then another batch with a different colour, and so on. Here's one way it's done:

① The fabrics are initially produced and <u>stored without dyeing</u>.

Batch of undyed fabric on roller

Dyed fabric collects on a second roller

③ The fabric is mounted on two <u>rollers</u> and is passed <u>back and forth</u> through the dye until all the dye is used up.

② When a batch of coloured fabric is needed, the <u>required amount</u> is dyed.

Dye vat

Fabric passes back and forth between rollers

④ The dyed fabric is put in a separate machine to <u>fix</u> the dye (to stop the colour from <u>running</u>) and to <u>wash off</u> excess dye.

2) Batch dyeing is useful because <u>fashionable colours</u> change quickly — so textiles <u>manufacturers</u> need to be able to <u>respond quickly</u>, and produce large <u>batches</u> of fabrics in <u>different colours</u>.

Colours can go out of fashion quickly.

Continuous Dyeing

1) In <u>continuous dyeing</u>, very <u>long lengths</u> of fabric are continuously passed through a small vat of dye.

2) The fabric is then passed between two <u>rollers</u>, which make sure the dye is <u>evenly spread</u> across the fabric and also remove any <u>excess</u>.

3) The dyed fabric is then <u>dried</u> and the dye <u>fixed</u>.

4) Continuous dyeing is useful for fabrics that <u>do not</u> need to <u>change colour</u> frequently with changing fashions.

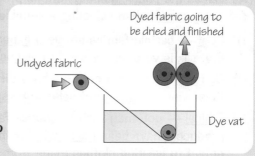

Dyed fabric going to be dried and finished

Undyed fabric

Dye vat

Printing Adds Colour to Specific Areas of a Fabric

1) <u>DISCHARGE PRINTING</u> is used to print a <u>lighter colour</u> onto a <u>dark fabric</u>. The dye is a <u>bleaching agent</u> (sometimes combined with a <u>coloured ink</u>). In the areas where the dye is applied, the dark colour is removed (and can be replaced with a new, lighter colour).

2) <u>RESIST PRINTING</u> is a method that uses paper or wax as a stencil (<u>resist</u>). Dye is applied to the fabric, but will <u>not colour</u> the areas that are covered by the stencil. Many <u>different stencils</u> can be used with <u>different coloured</u> dyes to create <u>complex patterns</u> and images.

3) <u>TRANSFER PRINTING</u> involves printing an image onto special <u>paper</u>. The paper is placed <u>face down</u> on the fabric and the design is <u>transferred</u> to the fabric by applying <u>heat</u> and <u>pressure</u> to the paper.

Finished this page alive — you'll live to dye another day...

Last night I discovered a new dye, it gives a nice bright orange colour, and I applied it in no time at all by just slopping it on my shirt — I think I'll call it <u>vindaloo beige</u>... I don't recommend trying it yourself though...

Dyeing and Printing

Roller Printing is Used To Print Continuous Patterns

Roller printing is used to print continuous patterns on very long pieces of fabric.

1) The design to be printed is engraved on a series of copper rollers — one for each colour needed.

2) The rollers are coated with dye as the fabric continuously runs under them and the engraved design is printed onto the fabric.

3) The dye is fixed to the fabric to stop it running using a chemical called a mordant (e.g. salt).

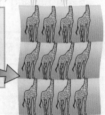

EXAM TIP:
If you're only asked to describe the process of roller printing, don't start giving advantages and disadvantages.

ADVANTAGES

1) It's a very quick and cost-effective method of printing once the rollers have been made.

2) Continuous patterns can be printed seamlessly.

DISADVANTAGES

1) The rollers are expensive and time-consuming to make.

2) The pattern can only be as big as the circumference of the roller.

Screen Printing can be Done by Hand or by Machines

1) Screen printing is an example of resist printing. It always uses some sort of screen and a squeegee.

2) In hand screen printing, the screen is a frame with fine mesh covering it.

3) A stencil is cut from card or acetate by hand or using CAD/CAM and put beneath the screen (on top of the fabric).

4) Printing ink is poured onto the screen, and a squeegee is drawn across the screen to force the ink through the mesh and the holes in the stencil.

5) The screen is lifted up and the design is left on the fabric.

6) In industry, the stencil is part of the screen and the squeegee is replaced by metal rods. The fabric is on a conveyor belt passing under different screens — one for each colour.

Squeegee
Mesh
Ink

Rotary screen printing

1) This is another method of industrial screen printing.

2) The screens are on cylinders — one for each colour

3) This is the quickest and most used method of commercial printing.

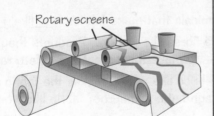
Rotary screens

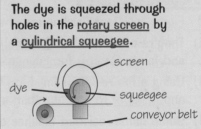
The dye is squeezed through holes in the rotary screen by a cylindrical squeegee.

screen
dye
squeegee
conveyor belt

Practice Questions

1) Suggest an advantage of batch dyeing compared to continuous dyeing.

2) How does discharge printing enable light colours to be printed onto dark fabric?

3) What is a mordant?

4) Robin is printing fabric for quilt covers with a stem and leaf design repeated continuously.
   a) Describe the difference between how the dye would be applied by roller printing and rotary screen printing.
   b) Which is the faster printing method — roller printing or rotary screen printing?

Fabric Finishes

Without finishes the world would be a mess — we'd all be creased, stained, soaking wet and some of us would be on fire. Hold tight — you're about to find out about the finishes that prevent all these things.

Finishes Improve The Performance of Fabrics

There are four reasons why finishes are used. They're all to do with changing something about the fabric.

1) To change the APPEARANCE of the fabric (e.g. sheen and colour).

2) To change the fabric's TEXTURE (e.g. smoothness and softness).

3) To change WEARING PROPERTIES (e.g. crease resistance, stain resistance).

4) To change AFTER CARE CHARACTERISTICS (e.g. shrinking).

Finishes are usually the last stage of fabric processing.

Some Finishing is Done Using Chemicals

Chemicals are applied to fibres or fabrics during manufacture to give fabrics beneficial properties.

WATER REPELLENT

1) Chemicals (e.g. silicones) can be applied to the surface of fabrics to stop water droplets getting through.

2) These finishes don't make the fabric waterproof — if the surface becomes saturated (completely covered in water) the water will leak through.

Nylon is often given a water repellent finish and used to make coats and tents.

STAIN RESISTANCE

1) Fabrics can be made stain resistant with a finish of a mixture of silicone and fluorine or a Teflon® coating.

2) These finishes stop grease and dirt from penetrating the fabric.

Stain resistant finishes are used a lot on carpets and upholstery.

ANTI-STATIC

1) When synthetic fabrics rub together, they can build up a static charge and cling to the wearer or give them slight electric shocks.

2) A finish can be applied to encourage the fabric to absorb small amounts of moisture from the atmosphere — this stops the static charge building up.

FLAME RESISTANCE

1) Flame resistant finishes are chemicals that make fabrics less likely to catch fire.

2) They're often used on flammable fibres like cotton. Products they're used on include nightclothes and fabric for soft furnishings — to make them meet fire safety requirements (see p.58).

3) Using a fire resistant finish on fabrics like cotton makes the fabric slightly stiffer, but it's still softer and cheaper to produce than a synthetic flameproof fabric like Nomex® (see p.28).

4) Some flame resistant finishes can be washed out, so care is needed when washing.

HYGIENIC

Antibacterial finishes can be applied to fabrics to prevent the growth of micro-organisms, which can cause infections or bad odours.

Hygienic finishes are applied to wound dressings, surgical masks and socks.

ROT PROOFING

1) Mildew can grow on fabrics made from natural fibres if they're kept in damp conditions.

2) Mildew growth can be reduced by applying a waterproof finish such as PVC to the fabric.

Fabric finish — is that the end of a sack race...

So you've finished this page — well done. You've learnt six finishes so far — another seven to go. When you're thinking about adding a finish, you need to balance the potential effects with the costs.

Fabric Finishes

A few more chemical finishes and then we'll finish off with some mechanical finishes. Sorry.

ANTI-PILLING

1) A pill is a small ball of fibres that's formed where a fabric has been rubbed.
    They're common on woollen and acrylic garments, e.g. jumpers and fleeces.

2) A polymer finish can be applied to the fabric, which stops loose fibres clumping together.

EASY CARE

1) These finishes are given to fabrics that crease easily (e.g. cotton and linen).

2) This means they need much less ironing.

ANTI-FELTING

1) These finishes are applied to woollen fabrics, which tend to shrink when washed.

2) Scales on wool fibres cause wool to shrink in the wash. Hot water and rubbing cause the fibres to move against each other and the scales tangle and lock together.

3) To stop this, the scales can be permanently removed with chlorine, or a coating applied to smooth the surface of the fibres.

Some Finishes are Applied *Mechanically*

The following are mechanical finishes — machines are used to create them. Mechanical finishes are cheaper to apply than chemical finishes, so won't increase the cost of the product too much.

Fabric brushing

1) Brushing fabric gives it a soft, raised surface . It's a permanent finish.

2) Fabrics are brushed by passing them between rollers covered with wire brushes to raise the surface.

3) The raised surface traps air and keeps the body warmer.

Calendering

1) Calendering makes fabrics smoother and shinier.

2) Heavy heated rollers are used to squash the fabric.

3) The finish is not permanent and wears off with time, but it's fairly durable.

Pre-shrinkage

1) Natural fibres which are prone to shrinking (e.g. wool and cotton) can be pre-shrunk.

2) This reduces further shrinkage when the fabrics are washed.

3) It's done by steaming the fabric on a vibrating conveyor belt.

Pleating

1) Pleating puts permanent creases into fabrics (see p.46).

2) Synthetic fabrics are heated and pressed using an edged roller — this melts the fabric and sets the pleat permanently (this is called heat setting).

3) To keep pleats in natural fabrics, a chemical finish is applied to the fabric before pressing.

Practice Questions

1) What are the four main reasons for applying a finish to a fabric?

2) Fred's overalls have a flame retardant finish.
    Why is it important that he follows the washing instructions carefully?

3) How can treatment with PVC prevent mildew from growing on a cotton product?

4) a) What are mechanical finishes?
    b) Give an advantage of using a mechanical finish rather than a chemical one.

Components

Unless you're making a flannel or a bed sheet, you're gonna need to use some components.

Components are Pre-manufactured Parts

1) Components are the bits and pieces that you use in addition to the fabric to make a textile product.

2) They can be functional, e.g. a zip to close your coat, or decorative, e.g. a lace edging.

Some Components are Fastenings

Fastenings are used to close products, or parts of products (like pockets).
They need to be suitable for the product and the intended user.

Parachute Clips

1) These are made from plastic or metal and are used as buckles on bags and belts.

2) They're very secure when fastened and can be unfastened quickly and easily.

3) They're quite bulky, so aren't suitable for products made from a delicate fabric.

Zips

1) These can be made out of plastic or metal, and be big and bulky or small and concealed (hidden) in your textile product.

2) Some zips are fixed at one end (e.g. on handbags). Zips on jackets are not fixed (so you can get the jacket off).

3) Zips with two sliders can be opened in two directions — the ends can be fixed (e.g. on suitcases) or open (e.g. on some jackets).

Hooks and Eyes

1) These are used to fasten bras and on the waistband of trousers and skirts (usually above a zip).

2) They make a secure and discrete fastening, which can be washed easily. However, they can snag delicate fabric.

Eyelets

1) These are metal rings used to reinforce a hole for passing a lace or ribbon through.

2) They're often found on lace-up shoes and bags or for making decorative fastenings on garments.

Toggles and Buttons

These are sewn on and require a buttonhole or a loop to fasten to.

They can be made of any hard material — plastic, metal, wood, and even glass.

They're easy to attach and replace, but can fall off, which makes them a choking hazard on children's products.

Velcro®

1) Velcro® comes in two halves — a rough tape and a smooth tape. Nylon hooks on the rough half attach to soft loops on the smooth half.

2) It takes quite a lot of force to open Velcro® — so it needs to be firmly attached to the fabric and isn't suitable for using with delicate fabrics.

Press studs (or poppers)

These can be used to fasten items that need to be opened and closed quickly. They can be made of metal or plastic and come in different sizes depending on the strength of fastening you require (bigger metal press studs are harder to open than small plastic press studs). And they're not very decorative.

Some fascinating fastening facts for you...

You need to know all about these fastenings so you can decide which are suitable for different products.

Components

You Can Use Other Components in Your Designs

1) **THREADS** can be used for joining fabric, securing other components or decorative stitching (see p.55).

2) They come in different thicknesses and textures. Sewing threads are thin and will form neat and strong seams. Embroidery threads can be thicker and have a variety of textures.

1) **INTERFACINGS** are extra layers of fabric hidden inside a product. They're used to give strength, stability and support. They come in different weights for different uses.

2) They're used in collars, cuffs, around button holes, and anywhere a product needs extra strength.

3) Some interfacings are 'fusible' — they stick onto materials when heated (e.g. by ironing). Bondaweb is a fusible double-sided interfacing used to bind fabrics together. It's used, for example, in appliqué (see p.54).

APPLIQUÉ MOTIFS are small fabric badges (often embroidered) that are sewn on to garments to add decoration. They can be used to show membership of clubs or teams.

1) **DECORATIVE ITEMS** include lace, ribbons, braid, ric-rac (wavy braid), laces, beads and sequins.

2) They're often used to add decoration around hems or pockets.

3) Ribbons, braids and laces can also be threaded through eyelets or holes to make a fastening. But they're often not very secure.

1) **SHOULDER PADS** are foam or quilted pads sewn into the lining of suit jackets or overcoats to give the impression that the wearer has broader shoulders.

2) They can be also be attached with velcro to make them removable.

3) Large shoulder pads were very popular in women's fashion in the 1980s, but they have since become less common and are now smaller and more discrete.

An 80s lady sporting some very fetching shoulder pads.

1) **CONSTRUCTION ITEMS** like pockets or cuffs can also be used to finish your products.

2) Pockets can either be functional or decorative. There's more about adding pockets on page 47.

3) Cuffs allow sleeves to be fastened and add weight to improve the drape of sleeve fabric.

Practice Questions

1) How might a zip on a coat be attached differently from a zip on a pair of trousers?

2) Suggest a suitable fastening for securing the top flap of a rucksack.

3) Alison is designing a cardigan that will be made using a delicate knitted fabric.
   a) Suggest a suitable fastening.
   b) What are the disadvantages of this type of fastening?

4) Bondaweb is a fusible interfacing.
   a) What are interfacings and why are they used?
   b) What does it mean if an interfacing is 'fusible'?

Tools and Equipment

There are lots of hand tools to get to grips with when you're manufacturing textiles products...

Use the Right Tools for the Job

FOR MARKING AND MEASURING

Use flexible **MEASURING TAPES** to accurately follow curved surfaces.

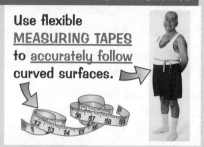

Use **TAILOR'S CHALK** to transfer markings onto your fabric that you can remove later, e.g. when you're marking out a pattern.

Use a **PATTERN MASTER** to help you draw paper patterns. Use the curved edge to mark out smooth curves and the parallel lines to mark out extra width for seam allowance.

FOR CUTTING

1) Use **PAPER SCISSORS** to cut out patterns.

2) Use **DRESSMAKING SCISSORS** (also called fabric shears) to cut fabric. These have long, very sharp blades that cut through fabric more easily and neatly.

3) Use **EMBROIDERY SCISSORS** for more delicate jobs, e.g. snipping threads, or clipping curved seams to help press them. They have short, sharp blades.

4) Use **PINKING SHEARS** to cut fabric with a zigzag edge — this helps prevent fabric from fraying.

Use **CRAFT KNIVES** to cut stencils (if, say, you want to spray a design onto fabric). You'll do a neater job than using scissors.

Use **SEAM RIPPERS** to unpick seams. Doing it by hand is slower, and scissors might accidentally cut the fabric.

FOR SEWING

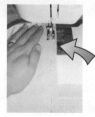

Use **PINS** to hold the fabric together before stitching with a sewing machine. Doing this means the fabric won't slip, and you can keep your fingers further away from the needle when you feed fabric through.

(For more safety tips see p.71.)

1) Use **NEEDLES** for hand stitching, e.g. embroidery, attaching beads to fabric, or tacking (see p.48).

2) Use a needle that's the right size for the thickness of the fabric and the thread you're using.

FOR PRESSING

1) **DRY IRONS** use heat and pressure to press creases out of fabric and flatten seams.

2) **STEAM IRONS** are more effective — they use water and steam as well as heat and pressure.

Do safety checks on irons before use, e.g. check for frayed cables — if you touch a live wire you could be electrocuted.

Irons have three heat settings:

Cool iron (1 dot) — for silk and for synthetics that melt.

Warm Iron (2 dots) — for mixed fabrics, but not synthetic fibres that melt.

Hot iron (3 dots) — for cotton and linen.

These symbols are on clothing labels.

Sewing — it seamed like a good idea at the time...

Naming suitable tools and equipment is a popular question in the exam. Make sure you know about all the tools on this page, including what they look like and why particular ones are suited to certain jobs.

Tools and Equipment

Use Sewing Machines to Join Fabrics

Sewing machines speed up sewing, and produce neat, even stitches for a high-quality finish.

MOST SEWING MACHINES ARE LOCKSTITCH MACHINES

They use two threads — one on a bobbin under the sewing plate, the other (the top thread) on the spool pin on top of the machine. The machine interlocks the two threads to make stitches.

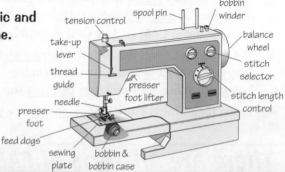

1) Before you start, choose the right needle for your fabric and thread thickness and fasten it securely into the machine.

2) It's a good idea to do some lines of stitching on a small sample of fabric first, so you can check:

   - that the thread tension is right. If the tension of the two threads is balanced then you'll get an even stitch, which isn't too tight or too loose.
   - that the stitch type and stitch length are correct.

Safety checks must be carried out before using a sewing machine, both at school and in industry.

- Make sure that the lead isn't a tripping hazard or frayed, and check that the plug isn't loose.
- Make sure that safety guards are in place.
- Know where the emergency stop button is (industrial sewing machines).

OVERLOCKERS CAN SEW SEAMS AND FINISH EDGES AT THE SAME TIME

1) Overlockers are used to finish edges to stop them from fraying. They do this by enclosing the edge, or edges, in a thread casing.

2) An overlocker works by using several top threads, but no bobbin. It also has a blade to trim the fabric edge before it's enclosed.

3) They can be used just to finish seam edges, or to sew, trim and neaten the seam all in one go.

4) They can be used for side seams in stretchy clothes like T-shirts.

Use Computerised Equipment to Add Embroidery

1) Embroidery (decorative stitching — see p.55) can be done by hand, with an ordinary sewing machine, or by using CAM (Computer-Aided Manufacture). There are a number of CAM sewing machines, e.g. the Janome Memory Craft and Pfaff® Creative.

2) CAM machines can stitch designs that are already programmed into the machine.

3) You can also use CAD software (see p.12-13) to produce your own designs — then save them onto a disk or memory card and transfer them to the CAM machine.

4) The fabric is secured in an embroidery hoop. The needle stays in one place while the machine moves the hoop around to create the design.

There's more on CAD/CAM on pages 42-43.

Practice Questions

1) a) What tool should you use to unpick seams, and why? b) What about cutting fabric?

2) How would you attach decorative beading to a handbag?

3) When you're using a sewing machine, what three things should you check on some sample fabric before starting the real thing?

4) Explain how you could use CAD/CAM to add decoration to a product.

Computerised Production

In industrial textiles production, most things are done by <u>big machines</u> — often <u>controlled by computers</u>.

CAD/CAM _is Used a Lot in_ Industry

1) <u>Computer-Aided Manufacture</u> (CAM) is the process of manufacturing products with the help of <u>computers</u>. Data is downloaded from a computer to a manufacturing machine — and this data controls the machine's processes.

2) <u>CAM</u> is usually <u>linked</u> with <u>CAD</u> (Computer-Aided Design, see p.13) — this is known as <u>CAD/CAM</u>. A product is <u>designed</u> using <u>CAD</u>, then information from the CAD software is used to <u>manufacture</u> the product using <u>CAM</u> (e.g. a CAD embroidery design is produced on a CAM embroidery machine).

3) The machines used in CAM are <u>Computer-Numerically Controlled</u> (CNC). This means they are sent <u>data</u> in the form of numbers. The machine's on-board processor <u>interprets</u> these numbers and <u>controls</u> the <u>movements</u> of the machine.

4) These days, most <u>industrial machines</u> are <u>CAM</u> machines...

EXAM TIP
Learn about the full range of CAM machines. You might be asked to explain how ICT could be used to help do something.

There are All Sorts of CAM Machines

CUTTING MACHINES

1) Before cutting, <u>many layers</u> of fabric are <u>automatically spread out</u> on the cutting table.
2) A <u>CAM cutting machine</u> cuts out the fabric pieces, following a <u>CAD lay plan</u> (see p.45).
3) The machine cuts through <u>all the layers</u> at once, which makes the cutting process <u>really quick</u> — this means a whole batch of fabric can be cut at once.
4) It cuts the fabric <u>accurately</u> at <u>high speed</u> using vertical knives, high-pressure water jets or lasers.

SEWING MACHINES

1) <u>Industrial</u> sewing machines are very strong as they need to work at <u>high speeds</u>. Different machines are <u>specially designed</u> for the <u>different</u> processes involved in making a product.
2) <u>CAM</u> sewing machines are used to carry out certain processes <u>automatically</u> — e.g. sewing buttonholes and attaching pockets.

EMBROIDERY MACHINES

1) <u>CAM embroidery machines</u> use <u>CAD</u> data to sew designs. They have many needles that change <u>automatically</u> as different coloured threads are needed.
2) <u>Computer control</u> makes these machines <u>very fast</u> and <u>accurate</u>, and the CAD <u>data</u> can be <u>quickly changed</u> to produce <u>new products</u>.

FABRIC PRINTERS

A <u>CAD</u> design can go directly from a computer to a <u>fabric printer</u> — the design is then printed <u>directly</u> onto the fabric. This is a <u>really quick</u> method of printing.

PLOTTER/CUTTERS — These machines use CAD data to <u>cut stencils quickly</u> and <u>accurately</u>.

PRESSING MACHINES

<u>Digital pressing machines</u> are used to improve the <u>appearance</u> of garments — they press fabric <u>flat</u> and flatten <u>seams</u> to finish the product <u>ready for sale</u>.

CAD/CAM — not a line dance where you flash your knickers...

Learn this page 'cause examiners have a nasty habit of asking about <u>how CAD/CAM is used in industry</u>.

Computerised Production

CAD/CAM *is Used to Make One-Off Items...*

1) <u>One-off</u> items are <u>unique</u> pieces, such as <u>models</u>, <u>prototypes</u>, <u>garments</u> made for a <u>specific person</u> and your <u>final product</u> for your <u>project</u>.

2) <u>CAD</u> can be used to <u>design</u>, and <u>develop</u> designs, for these items, and to <u>communicate</u> design ideas with a <u>client</u>. CAD can also be used to produce the <u>pattern</u> and a <u>lay plan</u>.

3) The manufacture of one-off items can be speeded up by using <u>CAM machines</u> — e.g. automated sewing machines and fabric printers.

A garment made by a top designer for a Hollywood star is a one-off item.

...And Large Quantities of a Product

1) CAM <u>speeds up</u> production processes — computer control means that processes can be done <u>automatically</u> (using CAD data), much <u>faster</u> than <u>people</u> could do them manually. This is really important for batch and mass production.

2) Machines controlled by computer are <u>more accurate</u> than if they were controlled by <u>people</u>, and processes are always done in <u>exactly the same way</u>. This means <u>consistent</u>, <u>higher quality</u> products and <u>less wastage</u>. Computers can be used to <u>monitor quality</u> too.

3) CAM machines don't need <u>people</u> to <u>control</u> them, just a few to <u>oversee</u> them, so they cut down on <u>labour costs</u>.

> All of the factors above mean that <u>large numbers</u> of <u>identical</u>, <u>high quality</u> products can be made <u>quickly</u> and <u>cheaply</u>.

CIM *is Computer-Integrated Manufacture*

<u>Computer-Integrated Manufacturing</u> (CIM) is when all the <u>individual</u> manufacturing <u>processes</u> (moving materials about, cutting, sewing, etc.) are <u>linked and controlled</u> by a computer system. This system <u>monitors</u> all the processes and keeps production going smoothly.

Databases *and* Spreadsheets *Help Too*

1) <u>Databases</u> are widely used in industry for <u>stock control</u>. For example, manufacturers might use a database to monitor how much <u>fabric</u> they have in stock, so they'll know when to order more.

2) <u>Spreadsheets</u> are another useful ICT tool — they can be used to <u>work out costs</u>, etc.

Practice Questions

1) What does <u>CAD/CAM</u> mean?

2) Explain how a <u>CAM cutting machine</u> makes cutting out pieces for textile products <u>very quick</u>.

3) Jo is designing a <u>one-off</u> ball gown for a wealthy Russian.
   Jo lives in Bognor Regis (in the UK).
   Describe how she can use <u>CAD</u> to get <u>instant feedback</u> on her design from her client.

4) Describe <u>two</u> ways in which CAD/CAM can <u>save</u> a manufacturer <u>money</u>.

5) Apart from CAD/CAM, <u>how else</u> are computers used in textile product manufacture?

Patterns

Patterns are usually made of tissue paper. You pin the pattern pieces to the fabric and cut around them to produce different shapes of fabric — which you can then sew together to make the textile product.

Patterns **Are** Templates **You** Cut Around

1) You'll need to make patterns for your projects. Designing clothing patterns from scratch is quite complicated so you might want to:

- Use an existing product as the basis for your own pattern — disassemble the product, look at the shape of each piece and make your own pattern based on these. You'll need to test your pattern (using cheap fabric) to make sure the pieces fit together the way you want them to.
- Use commercial patterns as a starting point — you can adapt them for your own design.

2) If you're making a garment, it's easiest to make it in your size, so you can try it on and alter it.

3) In industry, CAD is used in every step of pattern making — making it really quick and accurate. Here's how it's done:

> You might also get to use CAD to create pattern pieces for your designs.

- A pattern is drawn, checked and modified.
- Then it's graded — each piece is scaled up and down to make a set of patterns in different sizes.
- The best lay plan (see next page) is worked out. This data is then downloaded to a CAM cutting machine (see p.42) to cut out the pieces.

Pattern Symbols **Give** Detailed Instructions

Pattern pieces have markings that tell you how to cut and sew the pieces together to make the product.

Symbol	Meaning and Use
Grain Line ◁——▷	Shows the direction of the fibres/yarns so that the garment hangs properly and the fabric does not stretch in the wrong direction.
Place to fold ▽ ▽	The pattern must be placed against a fold to give a symmetrical fabric piece that's twice the size of the pattern piece when cut.
Cutting line ——	Shows where you must cut the fabric.
Stitching line - - - - -	Shows where to stitch the seam.
Darts ▷——• and ◁—•—▷	Show the location of the fold for a dart (see page 46).
Notches/ balance marks - - - - ▲	These are notches that are cut out within the seam allowance — they help you line up two pattern pieces correctly.
Buttons ⊛	The locations and sizes of these are given on pattern pieces.
Buttonholes ⊢——⊣	
Zips ◀□▾▴▾▴▾▴▾▴▸	

> Dots and circles are often found on patterns. They represent different things including places to start sewing, balance marks and points for using tailor tacks (see next page).

Example — a vest pattern...

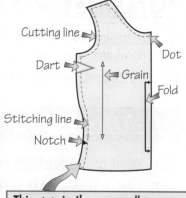

Cutting line ➤
Dart ➤
Dot
◁ Grain
Fold ➤
Stitching line ➤
Notch ➤

This gap is the seam allowance — often 1.5 cm.

Fabric patterns and no tartan, hoots mon ah dinny believe it...

In the exam you might get a pattern that you have to label with the pattern symbols. And you'll get no marks if you get them all muddled — so cover them up and scribble them out till you know every one.

Patterns

Pattern Markings **Can Be** Transferred **to the** Fabric

Before you remove the pinned pattern piece from the fabric you've cut out,
you need to transfer markings from the pattern to the fabric.

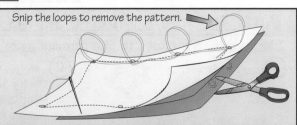

Snip the loops to remove the pattern.

TAILOR'S TACKS are double-threaded loose loops
sewn through the pattern and the layers of fabric
underneath. This method is good for marking a
double layer of fabric because you're left with tufts
of thread in both layers when you snip the threads
between them. (The tufts can be easily removed later.)

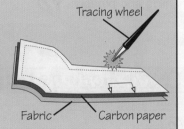

Tracing wheel

A **TRACING WHEEL** is used with
dressmakers' carbon paper.
The carbon paper is put between
the pattern and the fabric, and the
tracing wheel leaves a line of dots
on the fabric. These wash off
easily afterwards.

Fabric   Carbon paper

TAILOR'S CHALK (see page 40)
comes in different colours so that
you can choose one that shows
up against your fabric.
Tailor's pencils work the same way
as tailor's chalk but they come in
a convenient pencil shape.

Lay Plans — Arranging Pattern Pieces **on Fabric**

The pattern pieces are laid onto the fabric in the way that'll
waste the least fabric. CAD can be used to quickly work out
the most efficient lay plan.

Selvedge
Pattern piece
Fabric
Grain line

Different factors affect the design of the lay plan...

1) If a garment is being made in several different sizes, a multi-size lay plan might be best.
   This means putting pattern pieces for different sizes on the same fabric sheet —
   pieces from a small size might fit into the gaps between pieces from a larger size,

2) Fabric with checks, stripes or other designs needs to have the pattern pieces laid onto it so
   that the design faces the same way and seams match up. This can waste quite a lot of fabric.

3) The grain line on pattern pieces should usually be placed parallel to the fabric's selvedge.
   This is so all parts of the garment will stretch correctly.
   * Cut pile fabrics (see p.22) reflect light differently when viewed from different angles,
     so the pattern pieces can only be laid in one direction. This makes them wasteful fabrics.
   * Plain weave fabrics with no decoration (and many knitted fabrics) can have pieces laid in
     two directions — so they're more economical fabrics to use.
   * Non-woven fabric can have pieces laid in any direction to take up the least space.

4) In industry, there may be 50-80 layers of fabric being cut at once, so they can't use
   folded pieces. This means pattern pieces must show the entire shape of the product.

Practice Questions

1) Suggest two starting points you could use to avoid designing a clothing pattern from scratch.

2) What do these pattern symbols mean?   a) ▽   ▽   b) ▷   c) ⊢——⊣

3) What's the advantage of using tailor's tacks instead of chalk to mark out a pattern?

4) What is a multi-size lay plan?

5) Suggest a type of fabric that can have patterns laid out on it in:
   a) only one direction   b) two directions   c) any direction

Section Three — Tools and Processes

Construction Techniques

Jobs like sewing darts or attaching elastic can be <u>tricky</u>. Luckily, here's a page to <u>show you how</u>.

Disposal of Fullness Gets Rid of Excess Fabric

Here are a few ways to get rid of <u>excess fabric</u> — doing this creates <u>shape</u> in a product.

Darts Are Small, Tapered Seams That Take In Fabric

Triangular darts are used to <u>fit</u> a garment <u>more closely</u> to the body, e.g. at trouser waistlines.

(1) <u>Fold</u> the dart along the <u>centre</u> line...

(2) ...and <u>pin</u> the fold in place. <u>Stitch</u> along the line of the dart, starting from the <u>point</u>. Sew a few stitches <u>back</u> after you get to the edge of the fabric.

(3) Finally, <u>press</u> the dart to <u>flatten</u> it. You might need to <u>trim</u> the fold.

<u>Double ended darts</u> are used on fitted shirts and blouses.

They're made in a <u>similar</u> way to triangular darts, but they're <u>cut in the middle</u> before <u>pressing</u>.

Gathers Pull in the Fabric Evenly Along its Length

<u>Gathers</u> can be used at <u>waistbands</u>, <u>sleeve heads</u> or <u>cuffs</u>.

(1) <u>Knot</u> the threads at the start, or if machine sewing, leave a long thread that can be <u>wrapped</u> around a pin.

(2) Sew <u>two parallel rows</u> of stitches in the <u>seam allowance</u>. Use <u>small</u> <u>running stitches</u> when sewing by hand. If you're using a sewing machine, set the machine to its <u>longest stitch</u> and <u>loosest tension</u>.

(3) <u>Pull the threads</u> and ease the fabric along until it's drawn to the size you want.

Pleats and Tucks Are Folds in Fabric

Pleats — can be used to shape <u>skirts</u>.

1) Allow <u>three times</u> the finished width of fabric and <u>mark</u> the position of the pleats at <u>even widths</u> across the fabric.
2) <u>Fold</u> the pleats, <u>pin</u> them into position and <u>stitch</u> across the <u>top</u> of them to keep them in place.
3) <u>Pressing</u> gives the pleat <u>sharp creases</u>. Pressing <u>thermosetting fabrics</u> gives <u>permanent pleats</u>.

Tucks — can be used at <u>waistlines</u> or for <u>decoration</u>.

1) <u>Mark out</u> the position of the tucks.
2) <u>Fold</u> the tucks down and <u>machine stitch</u> along the fold to keep them in place.
3) <u>Press</u> the fabric flat and <u>repeat</u> with the next tuck.

tucks

stitching

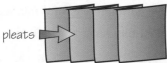
pleats

Tucks are narrower than pleats.

Drawstrings Can be Pulled to Gather Fabric

casing

A <u>casing</u> (channel of fabric) needs to be made to <u>thread</u> the drawstring through:

1) Fold and press a <u>double hem</u> (see p.50) which is <u>wider</u> than the <u>drawstring</u>.
2) Stitch along the <u>inner edge</u> of the hem, then along the <u>edge of the fabric</u> to form a <u>channel</u> with <u>stitching on both sides</u>.
3) <u>Thread</u> the drawstring <u>through the casing</u>, using a <u>safety pin</u> attached to one end (without pulling through the other end).

Elastic is For Places Where Stretch is Needed

Elastic can be <u>threaded</u> through a <u>casing</u> as for drawstrings (see above) or <u>machine-stitched</u> onto fabric.

Hand-sewn darts — you'll never score a bull's-eye with them...

Now you'll never get a pleat mixed up with a tuck again, never mind a gather. Thank goodness for that.

Construction Techniques

You Need to Know How to _Sew On Fastenings..._

Buttons

1) Sew them using a <u>strong thread</u>.
2) Repeat each stitch <u>seven or eight times</u>.

 Stitch buttons with <u>holes</u> either in parallel lines or a diagonal cross shape.

 Some buttons have a <u>shank</u> instead, where you sew through the hole and back into the fabric.

Buttonholes

Here's how you use a sewing machine to make a buttonhole:

1) Check the size of the button. Mark the position and length of the buttonhole.
2) Set the machine to a <u>half width zigzag</u> stitch and machine one side of the buttonhole.
3) Lift the presser foot, change to <u>full width zigzag</u> and machine a <u>bar tack</u> at the end of the buttonhole.
4) Turn the fabric round and repeat these 2 stages to complete the buttonhole edging.
5) Finally, make a <u>slit</u> for the button to go through.

Zips

1) Zips can be <u>open-ended</u> (e.g. on the front of a jacket) or <u>fixed</u> (e.g. on a pocket in a bag).
2) To make sewing the zip in easier, first <u>tack</u> along the <u>seam line</u> in which you want to insert the zip. Then press the seam open.
3) Place the zip <u>wrong-side-up</u> over the seam and <u>stitch</u> into place.
4) Now just <u>remove</u> the tacking and it's done.

For a fixed zip, <u>stitch across</u> the ends.

...and _Pockets_

1) The most common sort are <u>patch pockets</u> — they're sewn onto the <u>front</u> of a product.
2) <u>Cut out</u> a piece of <u>fabric</u> that's the size and shape of the pocket plus seam allowance.
3) <u>Turn over</u> the <u>top</u> edge to form a <u>hem</u> and <u>stitch</u> it in place.
4) <u>Press</u> the <u>hem</u>, then fold over the <u>other three edges</u> and press them too.
5) Position and <u>pin</u> the pocket on the product. Then stitch it in place all round the edge, <u>reinforcing</u> the top corners with a triangle of stitching to secure them.

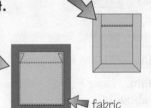

hem

fabric

Pockets can also be put into <u>seams</u> to <u>hide</u> them (e.g. trouser side pockets).

Practice Questions

1) Describe how to put a <u>dart</u> into a piece of fabric.

2) Describe the difference between <u>pleats</u> and <u>tucks</u>.

3) Paul collects chopsticks, and is going to make a bag to keep them in. Suggest <u>two closing techniques</u> that will hold his chopsticks securely.

4) If you were making a pencil case, would you need a <u>fixed</u> or <u>open-ended</u> zip?

5) Sarah wants a square pocket with sides of <u>5 cm</u> on the front of her apron. She carefully cuts a square of fabric with sides of exactly <u>5 cm</u>. What mistake has Sarah made?

Joining Fabric

Ah, welcome to the calm pages of fabric harmony — it's all about joining them together...

Pin or Tack to Join Fabrics Together Temporarily

line you're going to sew along

Fabrics can slip when you're trying to machine or hand sew them together, so it's best to pin or tack them in place first.

- **PINNING** — put pins at right angles to the edge of the fabric.
- If you're machine sewing, remove the pins as you come to them.

- **TACKING** (sometimes called basting) involves hand sewing long running stitches (about 1 cm). Do these in a different colour from the fabric, so you can easily see them.
- Tacking holds the fabric together more securely than pinning (it's best to pin before tacking though).
- Once you've tacked, remove all the pins, then you can see what your pieces will look like when joined.
- Stitch over your tacking and then remove the tacking stitches.

If your fabric will be damaged by pinholes or by tacks, e.g. PVC-coated or leather fabrics, you could use paperclips or bulldog clips to hold it in place instead.

Seams Join Pieces of Fabric Together Permanently

Seams need to hold fabric securely and be strong enough to stand up to the strains put on the product. There are different types you can use, depending on the fabric and use of the product.

Plain (Open) Seam — Easy to do

1) To make a plain seam, take two pieces of fabric and put the right sides together. Then pin or tack to hold the fabric in place.
2) Stitch 1.5 cm in from the edge of the fabric (patterns have a seam allowance to allow extra fabric for this).
3) Strengthen the seam by reversing back over it for a few centimetres at both ends of the seam.
4) Open out the seam and iron so it lies flat.

stitching

- Plain seams look neat on the outside — you can only see a thin joining line.
- But they're only used for joins that aren't going to be under too much strain.

Double-Stitched Seam — a Strong Seam

1) To make a double-stitched seam, first stitch a plain seam (see above).
2) Press the seam open and trim one side to 5 mm.
3) Fold the uncut edge over the cut edge.
4) Press the seam over to the side and stitch it flat to the fabric (use a zigzag stitch if you want a decorative finish).
5) Press the seam flat.

seam edges

stitching

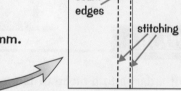

See page 50 for how to neaten edges.

- Double-stitched seams are used where strength is needed, e.g. jeans.
- But they're too bulky for delicate fabrics.

You tacking to me — well it certainly seams that way...

As you'll have gathered, seams are pretty important in textiles and in life in general. But often you can't just use any old one — you have to think about which one is best. So no 'overlocking' these pages...

Joining Fabric

And Then There's the French and Overlocked Seams

French Seam — Hides the Seam Edges

1) Place the fabrics the <u>wrong</u> sides together, then pin and tack.

2) <u>Stitch</u> 8 mm from the edge of the fabric and then <u>trim</u> this down to 3 mm.

3) <u>Fold</u> the fabric over — so the <u>right</u> sides are together
   and the seam is on the edge of the fabric.

4) Stitch the fabric 7 mm from the edge, so that the raw edge is totally <u>enclosed</u>.

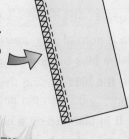

- French seams are used for <u>fine</u>, <u>sheer fabrics</u> or fabrics that are <u>likely to fray</u>.
  They're good for <u>baby clothes</u> as there are no rough edges to irritate the skin.

- But they can be <u>bulky</u> if used on thicker fabrics.

Overlocked Seam — Quick to do

1) Place the fabrics the <u>right</u> sides together, then pin and tack.

2) An <u>overlocking machine</u> is used to <u>encase the edges</u> of the fabric.
   See p.41 for more on how it does this and a beautiful picture of one.

3) You can use an overlocker to <u>sew, trim and finish edges</u> all in one go
   — so it's a <u>very quick way</u> to do seams. But they <u>trim</u> at the same
   time as sewing, so be careful to sew in the right place.

- Overlocked seams are <u>strong</u> and <u>quick</u> to do.

- They're good for <u>stretchy</u> clothes like T-shirts
  because they 'give' slightly with the fabric.

EXAM TIP
If you're asked to explain how
to do one of these seams in
the exam, you might want to
draw a diagram to help you.

Practice Questions

1) There are two common methods of joining fabric together <u>temporarily</u>.

   a) Name these methods.

   b) Give an advantage and a disadvantage of each.

2) Give <u>one advantage</u> and <u>one disadvantage</u> of using a <u>plain</u> seam to join fabric.

3) How wide is a <u>seam allowance</u> for a plain seam usually?

4) How could you make a <u>double seam</u> more decorative?

5) Describe how to do a <u>French seam</u>.

6) Suggest which <u>seam type</u> you would use for:

   a) a rugby shirt

   b) a silk dress

   c) cotton/LYCRA® leggings

7) Why would it be a disaster if you did an <u>overlocked seam</u> in the
   wrong place on your almost-complete product?

Neatening and Finishing

It doesn't matter how useful your product is, you need to make sure it looks the part too...

Neatening Edges Makes Your Product Look Better

You need to neaten all the raw edges of your product to make sure they don't fray.
There are several ways of doing this...

The simplest method for woven fabric is to cut a zigzag edge using `PINKING SHEARS`. This helps to stop the threads from unravelling, but it isn't enough for fabrics that are likely to fray badly.

You can neaten a seam edge by turning it under and machine sewing it — like a little hem.

You can also sew a line of zigzag stitches along the seam allowance and then trim as close as you can to the stitches.

You could use an `OVERLOCKER` to encase your edges (see page 41) — although an overlocker will trim the edges as well, so don't overlock the wrong bit or your work will be ruined.

You can use `BIAS BINDING` to neaten seam edges. Here's what you do...

1) Make a normal plain seam.
2) Fold the bias binding in half along its length.
3) Place the bias binding over the edge of the fabric to enclose it, then pin and tack in place.
4) Sew it in place using a normal straight machine stitch.

Bias binding is a strip of fabric with the edges pressed under. It's slightly stretchy, so it's great for neatening curved seams.

Seams can also be encased with bias binding on the outside of the product to make them decorative.

`FACINGS` can be used to neaten an awkward-shaped edge, e.g. round the armhole of a sleeveless garment. The facing might be cut from the same material or from a lighter-weight material.

1) Cut a piece of the facing material about 5 cm wide with the same shape as the edge that needs facing.
2) Pin and tack the facing to the edge of the product with the right sides together.
3) Machine along the seam line as normal.
4) If the seam is curved, cut notches into the seam allowance so it lies flat.
5) Press the facing carefully inside the product. You might need to secure it with a few small stitches.

`HEMS` are used to finish the raw edges of a product, e.g. the bottoms of skirts or sleeves. The fabric is folded over — once for a single hem and twice for a double or rolled hem — and then stitched.

1) The fold needs to be the right size for the size and weight of the product.
2) Pin and tack the fabric in the right position first.
3) Use the same colour thread so it blends in (unless you want it to stand out).

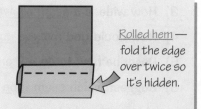

Rolled hem — fold the edge over twice so it's hidden.

Rolled hem — great in sandwiches...

This is where you tidy people get to be very precise about your product, and pick up extra marks for making it all lovely. Even if this isn't your thing, it's good stuff to know for the exam — so get learnin'.

Neatening and Finishing

Finish Products by Pressing

Every time that you sew a seam, you should press it. This is different from ironing — you don't iron the whole part of the product, just over where you've been working.

1) Use the right temperature for the type of fabric you're using (see page 40). If you're not sure, try it on a scrap piece of the same fabric first. Start with a cool iron and gradually make it hotter, till the right finish is achieved.

2) Some fabrics should be ironed dry and some can be ironed with a steam iron.

3) Some fabrics, like wool, are better pressed with a pressing cloth (a piece of cloth to protect the product from direct heat) so that the iron doesn't leave the shape of its sole plate on the fabric.

4) Awkward bits, like sleeves, can be ironed using a sleeve board — it's like a mini-ironing board.

5) Where you're pressing over a curve, such as where a sleeve meets the shoulder, you can use a curved shape called a tailor's ham to give you the firm surface that you need underneath.

> When you've finished making your product, you need to make sure that there are no creases where there shouldn't be and that all corners are sharp — you might need to iron or steam the whole thing again. Also, check all of the seams and hems to make sure that there are no loose threads hanging anywhere — if there are, trim them to give a neat and tidy finish.

Pressing Techniques are Used in Industry Too

Different pressing techniques are used in industry, for example...

- Under-pressing neatens the seams before adding a hem.

- Top-pressing is done at the very end to finish the product ready for sale — it's basically just giving the clothing a really good steam iron.

- Steam dollies can be used to remove creases in clothing. The clothes are put on a body-shaped doll, which is then inflated with steam. This helps press awkward-shaped products like skirts and dresses.

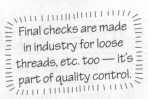

Final checks are made in industry for loose threads, etc. too — it's part of quality control.

- Tunnel finishers are used for shirts and blouses — the product is put on a hanger and passed through a tunnel, where it's steamed and dried.

Practice Questions

1) You can finish raw seam edges with pinking shears or by turning the edge under and sewing. Give an advantage and a disadvantage of each of these methods.

2) You've made a pair of oven gloves. Suggest how you could finish the seams so they'd look neat and decorative.

3) A facing is sometimes used to neaten an edge.
   a) What sort of edge would you neaten with a facing?
   b) Describe how you use a facing.

4) How do you decide how big a hem should be?

5) Name two pieces of equipment that you might use for ironing your product (other than the iron and ironing board). Explain what each is used for.

6) Describe two special pieces of equipment that are using for industrial pressing.

Colouring Fabric

Well here they are, the fabric colouring pages — I bet you've been dyeing to get started on these...

Dyeing is Used to Apply Colour to Fabric

1) <u>Natural</u> fibres, like cotton, wool and silk, are the <u>best</u> for dyeing as they're very <u>absorbent</u>.

2) The <u>colour of the fabric</u> you begin with makes a difference to the final colour — for example if you dye <u>white fabric red</u>, you get <u>red fabric</u> — if you dye <u>yellow fabric red</u>, you get <u>orange</u>.

3) Fabrics that have an <u>uneven colour</u> need to be <u>bleached</u> before dyeing to ensure an even final colour.

4) For some fabrics and dyes, you need to use a chemical called a <u>mordant</u> (e.g. salt) to <u>fix</u> the colour to the fabric. This makes the fabric <u>colourfast</u> — the dye won't come out in the wash.

5) One of the <u>advantages</u> of <u>hand</u> dyeing is that you can add <u>designs</u> to the fabric using a 'resist'. A '<u>resist</u>' is something that <u>prevents the dye</u> from reaching the <u>fabric</u>.

Tie Dye is Easy to Do

1) Fabric is <u>tied</u> with <u>string</u> or <u>rubber bands</u> to create a <u>resist</u>.

2) The fabric is then <u>immersed</u> in dye.

3) The dye <u>doesn't get to</u> the tied areas.

This vest has been tie dyed.

4) Once the dye has <u>dried</u> and the fabric is <u>untied</u>, the pattern is <u>revealed</u>.

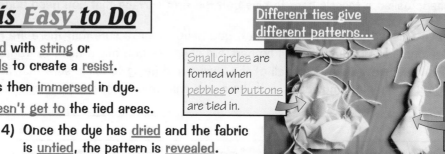

Different ties give different patterns...

<u>Small circles</u> are formed when <u>pebbles</u> or <u>buttons</u> are tied in.

Concertina <u>pleats</u> give <u>parallel lines</u>.

Tying the fabric out from the <u>centre</u> produces a '<u>sunburst</u>' effect.

ADVANTAGES
1) Every piece will be <u>unique</u>.
2) The <u>equipment</u> is <u>cheap</u> and <u>readily available</u>.
3) It's an <u>easy</u> way to <u>add a pattern</u> to fabrics.

DISADVANTAGES
1) The outcome is <u>unpredictable</u>.
2) You <u>can't repeat</u> a pattern exactly.
3) You can't create a <u>detailed pattern</u>.
4) It's <u>time consuming</u> for <u>large</u> areas.

Batik — Good For More Detailed Designs

In <u>batik</u> the resist used is usually <u>hot wax</u>.

1) The fabric is stretched across a <u>frame</u>. Then the <u>hot wax</u> is applied with a <u>brush</u> or a <u>tjanting</u> (pointed tool for dripping the wax) to create a pattern.

2) Once the wax has set, the dye is <u>painted</u> on, or the fabric can be immersed in a <u>dye bath</u>.

3) The wax is <u>ironed</u> off to reveal the pattern.

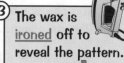

ADVANTAGES
1) It's a more <u>precise</u> way of adding <u>patterns</u> to fabrics than tie dye.
2) <u>Patterns</u> can be <u>more detailed</u>.
3) Every product will be <u>unique</u>.

DISADVANTAGES
1) It's <u>time consuming</u> — each part of the design has to be painted separately.
2) You need to be <u>careful</u> when working with <u>hot wax</u>, and it's easily dripped in the <u>wrong</u> place.
3) It can be <u>tricky</u> to iron all the <u>wax out</u>.

Nice tie — thanks, I couldn't resist...

Tie dying was all the rage when I was young — it's a great way of giving old clothes a new lease of life. Just remember to tie the string tight enough, otherwise it doesn't work (oops).

Colouring Fabric

Block Printing *is Used to Apply a* Design *to* Fabric

1) Printing is the process of applying <u>ink</u>, <u>dye</u> or <u>paint</u> to fabric in <u>defined patterns</u>.

2) Fabrics with a <u>plain weave</u> are best for printing on, because they have a <u>smooth surface</u> for the dye to be applied to and <u>no surface pattern</u> to <u>detract</u> from the design.

3) To do block printing, you need to use a <u>printing block</u> with a <u>raised design</u>:

- Make one by <u>drawing</u> a pattern on a piece of <u>wood</u> and then <u>cutting</u> the <u>background away</u>, leaving the design <u>raised</u>. The pattern must be a <u>mirror image</u> of the print you want.
- Or you can <u>stick</u> pieces of <u>card</u> or <u>string</u> onto a solid <u>block</u>.
- You can also <u>buy rubber blocks</u> with designs already on them.

<u>The printing process...</u>

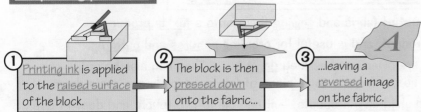

① <u>Printing ink</u> is applied to the <u>raised surface</u> of the block.

② The block is then <u>pressed down</u> onto the fabric...

③ ...leaving a <u>reversed</u> image on the fabric.

ADVANTAGES

1) You can use <u>several blocks</u> to build up a more <u>complicated</u> design.
2) You can easily <u>repeat</u> designs.
3) You can use the same block <u>many</u> times before it <u>wears out</u>.

DISADVANTAGES

1) <u>Making</u> the blocks takes a <u>long time</u>.
2) It's not good for <u>fine detail</u>.

In industry, <u>engraved rollers</u> are used instead of blocks. The rollers are inked as the fabric is <u>continuously</u> run under them. This is fast but the rollers are <u>expensive</u> to make, so it's only cost-effective for large amounts of fabric.

Diffusers Spray Colour *onto* Fabric

<u>Dye</u> can be applied to fabric with a <u>diffuser</u>:

1) <u>Dampen</u> the fabric so that the dye will be <u>absorbed easily</u>.
2) Place a <u>stencil</u> of the shape that you want over the fabric.
3) Gently <u>spray</u> the fabric with the dye from the <u>diffuser</u>.
4) <u>Iron</u> to set the dye.

Diffusing gives an <u>even effect</u> all over the fabric — or you can make it <u>heavier</u> in places where you want it <u>darker</u>. You can also use several colours on top of each other so that they <u>blend</u> together.

Practice Questions

1) In the dyeing process, explain why a fabric might need to be:
   a) <u>bleached</u>
   b) treated with a <u>mordant</u>

2) James is trying to dye a star and turtle pattern onto some <u>polyester</u> fabric.
   a) Suggest a suitable method of <u>hand dyeing</u> he could use.
   b) Explain how James could produce <u>better</u> results by using a <u>different</u> fabric.

3) Maurice wants to produce bags with a <u>handmade</u> appearance, featuring a <u>simple</u> printed design.
   a) Suggest a <u>printing method</u> he could use.
   b) Give <u>one advantage</u> and <u>one disadvantage</u> of this printing method.

4) Ali wants to make a quilt cover based on this photo of a sunset.
   Explain how she could <u>apply the dye</u> for the sky.

Decorating Fabric

Time to make your product more interesting with a <u>surface embellishment</u> (...or decoration to you and me).

Quilting uses Wadding Between Layers

1) <u>Quilting</u> uses <u>wadding</u> between <u>two layers</u> of fabric which are then <u>stitched together</u> in <u>straight lines</u> or in a <u>pattern</u>.

2) Quilting is often used to give added <u>warmth</u> to a product, e.g. an anorak or a bed cover. The wadding <u>traps warm air</u> between the <u>layers</u> of fabric.

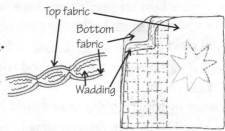
Top fabric
Bottom fabric
Wadding

Appliqué is Sewing Bits of Fabric On Top

1) Appliqué involves <u>cutting shapes</u> out of fabric and <u>sewing</u> them onto a <u>textile product</u>.

2) It adds <u>texture</u> and <u>colour</u> to a product, and is useful for creating <u>pictures</u> and <u>patterns</u>.

3) <u>Non-woven</u> fabrics, such as felt, are often used as they <u>don't fray</u>. They can also be <u>cut in any direction</u> — so <u>more shapes</u> can be cut from a single piece of fabric, which keeps costs down.

4) Appliqué is popular for decorating <u>children's</u> products — it can be <u>soft</u> to touch, and doesn't use any <u>dangerous small pieces</u>.

1) <u>Position</u> the cut shape on the fabric and <u>keep it in place</u> using pins, tacking stitches or a fusible interface like bondaweb (see p.39).

2) The use of <u>bondaweb</u> can also add <u>bulk</u>, stop the appliqué from <u>stretching</u> when it's being <u>sewn</u> and prevent woven fabric from <u>fraying</u>.

3) <u>Fraying</u> can also be prevented by <u>folding</u> the edges of the shape under before stitching.

4) Machine stitch the design. A <u>close zigzag</u> stitch is usually used — or <u>different stitches</u> can be used for other effects.

Bottom fabric
Top fabric

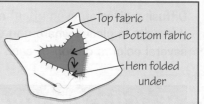

<u>Coloured thread</u>, sequins or beads can be used for added <u>decorative</u> effect.

Padded appliqué
Top fabric
Wadding
Bottom fabric

Place <u>wadding</u> or <u>stuffing</u> between the fabric pieces to create a <u>3D effect</u>.

Reverse appliqué
<u>Holes</u> are cut out of the <u>main fabric</u> and the appliqué is sewn on <u>behind</u> the hole on the <u>inside</u> of the product.

Top fabric
Bottom fabric
Hem folded under

ADVANTAGES OF APPLIQUÉ
1) It <u>strengthens</u> the base fabric because it makes a <u>double layer</u>.
2) <u>Shapes</u> can be <u>repeated accurately</u> if templates are used.
3) It allows <u>scraps</u> of fabric to be <u>used</u> rather than being wasted.
4) It can be sewn <u>automatically</u> using **CAM** machines.

DISADVANTAGES
1) It takes a lot of <u>extra material</u>.
2) It adds <u>thickness</u> and <u>weight</u> to products.

Whoops...I forgot to sew on the reverse appliqué...

Appliqué — a bit patchy when it comes to comedy material...

You can <u>use</u> some of these techniques in your designs — they can really help to <u>spice up</u> your product. And any of them could be in the exam — so <u>test yourself</u> by matching the names to the techniques.

Decorating Fabric

Embroidery _is_ Decorative Stitching

1) Embroidery is decorative stitching — it can be done by hand or machine.
2) Different types of thread give different textures and finishes,
   e.g. silk will give a shiny finish. Lots of different stitches can be used.
3) CAM embroidery machines can be used to automatically produce designs.

Examples of Embroidery Stitches
Chain stitch 
Herringbone stitch
Blanket stitch

ADVANTAGES
1) Can do very intricate patterns.
2) Adds texture as well as colour.

DISADVANTAGES
1) Can be easily damaged.
2) Very time consuming and expensive if done by hand.

HAND EMBROIDERY is done using a needle and thread.
1) The fabric is ironed, then it's stretched and secured in an embroidery hoop or frame.
2) The design is then pencilled on or drawn onto the fabric using tailor's chalk.
3) The pattern is sewn using different decorative stitches.

FREE MACHINE EMBROIDERY is done using a sewing machine.
1) The fabric is prepared as for hand embroidery, but put into an 'upside down' hoop
   — so that the fabric can lie flat on the machine.
2) The feed dogs (which push the fabric in a straight line when stitching normally) are lowered
   or covered in order to allow the fabric to be moved freely in any direction whilst sewing.
3) The presser foot is replaced with a darning foot and different stitches are selected.

After the embroidery is finished the fabric's removed from the embroidery hoop,
lose threads are cut off and it's ironed.

Patchwork _is Fabric made from Lots of_ Smaller Pieces

Patchwork is putting together different pieces of fabrics to make one big piece of fabric.
1) English or hand pieced patchwork can be made up of squares, triangles, hexagons,
   or any other shapes that will tessellate (fit together without leaving any spaces).
2) American or machine pieced patchwork is made up of squares, rectangles and
   triangles, which are sewn together on a sewing machine using 5 mm seams.

Beads _and_ Sequins _are Useful Pre-Manufactured Items_

Beads and sequins can be sewn
on by hand to add decoration...

They add colour,
and texture.

They also reflect light
in interesting ways.

...you can also buy sequined material.

Practice Questions

1) a) Name the technique used to apply this flower decoration.
   b) Suggest two ways to prevent the decoration from fraying.

2) a) What is the main purpose of embroidery?
   b) Give one disadvantage of using embroidery to decorate a product.
   c) How would you prepare fabric for embroidery?
   d) How would you prepare a sewing machine for free machine embroidery?

3) Explain the difference between patchwork and quilting.

Social and Cultural Issues

When you're designing, you should take into account the needs of a wide variety of people.

Designers Need to Think About the Needs of...

1 ...People of Different Sizes...

1) People come in lots of different shapes and sizes and they all need clothes to fit.

2) Anthropometric data gives average sizes for people (see p.14), but designers also need to think about people who don't fit those average sizes.

3) For example, tall people need their clothes (including footwear) in a longer length, and plus size people require larger sizes, wider-fitting shoes and different patterns to suit their shape.

4) A designer must take these needs into account when designing for a specific target group.

5) Some companies design and make clothes for people with sizes above or below the average, e.g. Long Tall Sally stocks clothes and shoes for tall women, so their shoe sizes go up to a size 11.

> They never stock clothes in my size...

2 ...People in Different Age Groups...

People in different age groups have different physical limitations and so need different things from their clothes. For example:

Loose button eyes on a teddy are a choking hazard.

1) Older people may feel more comfortable in looser, less-restrictive clothing — e.g. clothes made of light material or that have elasticated waistbands.

2) Small children need textile products that are safe — e.g. toys with components that won't fall off and non-flammable nightwear.

3 ...and People with Disabilities

People with disabilities may have specific needs from textiles products, especially clothing, e.g:

1) Some people need help from a carer to dress, so they need clothes that are easy to get on and off, e.g. a blouse that opens at the back.

2) Some people have problems with small or complicated fastenings like zips or buttons, so they need easy-to-open and close fastenings such as Velcro® or magnet fastenings.

3) Some people may find it difficult to look after clothes with special care instructions, e.g. 'dry clean only' or 'hand wash'. They need easy-care clothes — that are easy to wash and dry, and need little or no ironing.

The buttons on this jacket may be hard for some people to open. Velcro could be put under the buttons, which is easier to open but maintains the look.

- There are companies that specialise in clothes for disabled people — some sell specially adapted clothes (e.g. Adaptawear) and others make one-off products specifically designed for the user.

- These clothes are often more expensive because they aren't mass produced (see p.64).

The needs of a student revising: pen, paper, chocolate, gorilla...

When designing a textile product, you need to think about the specific requirements of your target group. If you fulfil the needs of your target group, your product is more likely to sell.

Social and Cultural Issues

A designer also needs to take into account different people's <u>views</u> and <u>cultural backgrounds</u>.

Not Everyone <u>Sees a Product in the</u> Same Way

1) You might think that a T-shirt with a particular <u>slogan</u> is really <u>funny</u> or <u>fashionable</u>, but other people might <u>disagree</u> or even be <u>offended</u>.

2) When you design a product you need to think about <u>opposing viewpoints</u> like these and try to make sure that your product has a mainly <u>positive</u> impact on society.

3) The <u>wider</u> your <u>target market</u>, the <u>more views</u> you need to consider — e.g. there are now <u>global markets</u> (see p.5).

Culture <u>is a Way of Life</u>

1) The <u>culture</u> of a particular <u>country</u> or <u>group of people</u> covers everything from their <u>religion</u>, <u>beliefs</u> and <u>laws</u> to their <u>language</u>, <u>food</u>, <u>dress</u>, <u>art</u> and <u>traditions</u>.

2) Examples of traditional dress include <u>saris</u> worn by <u>Indian</u> women, and <u>kimonos</u> worn in <u>Japan</u>. Designers need to think about <u>traditional styles</u> worn by their <u>target market</u>, and how their <u>lifestyle</u>, <u>climate</u> etc. affects the <u>suitability</u> of designs.

3) The <u>traditional clothing</u> of different cultures also <u>influences</u> the design of <u>modern</u>, <u>Western</u> textile products. For example, cowboy hats/boots, tartan skirts, tribal patterns and kaftans are all seen on the catwalk and in high street shops.

4) The <u>processes</u> involved in making traditional clothing also influence Western textile products. For example, <u>batik</u> (see p.52) is a technique that has been used in <u>Indonesia</u> for centuries and is now popular in Western textile designs.

Designers <u>Must Be Aware of the</u> Feelings <u>of Others</u>

1) If you're designing a product aimed at a <u>specific</u> target market, you'll have to take into account the <u>views and feelings</u> of people from that particular culture, because certain <u>symbols</u>, <u>images</u>, <u>colours</u> and <u>styles</u> can put people off buying a product.

2) For example, the <u>misuse</u> or <u>abuse</u> of <u>religious symbols</u> on textile products will <u>offend</u> some people.

3) If you want to sell your product <u>globally</u>, then you're going to have to take into account the <u>views</u> of as many <u>different cultures</u> as possible. This might mean you have to <u>adapt</u> your design.

4) For example, <u>showing bare skin</u> or using <u>transparent fabrics</u> in garments may <u>offend</u> people in some cultures. You could <u>adapt</u> garments for these markets by making them <u>longer</u>, adding <u>sleeves</u> or using <u>opaque</u> fabric.

Some cultures have more revealing dress than others.

Practice Questions

1) Dan's designing some trousers for <u>tall</u> people. How will his design be <u>influenced</u> by his target market?

2) Shane wants to produce some clothes specifically for <u>older people</u>.
   a) Suggest two features that the clothes might have to make sure that they are <u>comfortable</u>.
   b) Suggest a feature he should <u>avoid</u> and explain why.

3) Give an example of traditional clothing from another culture that's seen in UK <u>high street shops</u>.

4) Give an example of a design feature that might <u>offend</u> people and explain why this is offensive.

Safety and Moral Issues

Designers and manufacturers have a <u>moral</u> and <u>legal</u> responsibility to make sure their products are <u>safe</u>.

A Designer Must Choose Safe Materials

When designing you need to think about the product's <u>function</u> and <u>who's going to use it</u> — this will help you pick appropriate <u>materials</u> and <u>components</u> to make it <u>safe</u>.

Ask yourself some <u>questions</u> like these...

1) **Have I chosen <u>materials</u> and <u>components</u> suitable for the intended <u>function</u>?**
   E.g. is the fabric you've selected for protective clothing strong enough?

2) **Have I chosen <u>materials</u> and <u>components</u> suitable for the intended <u>user</u>?**
   E.g. use Velcro® fastenings instead of buttons (choking hazard) on clothes for small children.

3) **Are the <u>dyes</u> or <u>paints</u> you're using safe?** E.g. make sure that dyes used on children's toys/clothes are non-toxic as children are likely to put the products in their mouths.

4) **Are the <u>fabrics flammable</u>?** E.g. make nightclothes out of polyester (low flammability) rather than cotton (high flammability).

There Are Laws to Protect Product Users

Manufacturers who produce <u>unsafe</u> or <u>unreliable</u> products are probably <u>breaking</u> one of these <u>laws</u>:

1) The <u>General Product Safety Regulations</u> state that <u>manufacturers</u> are <u>responsible</u> for the <u>safety</u> of their products. They have to put <u>warnings</u> on any textile products that might be <u>hazardous</u>. For example, a toy with button eyes that a small child could choke on must have a warning such as 'NOT SUITABLE FOR CHILDREN UNDER 3 YEARS'.

2) The <u>Furniture and Furnishings (Fire Safety) Regulations</u> cover upholstered furniture and cushions, etc. They say that all <u>fabrics</u> used to cover <u>furniture</u> must be <u>resistant</u> to catching fire from matches and other materials (e.g. stuffing) mustn't catch fire from <u>smouldering cigarettes</u>.

3) The <u>Consumer Protection From Unfair Trading Regulations</u> state that any <u>claims</u> made about a product (e.g. that it is hard-wearing, long-lasting, waterproof) must be <u>true</u>.

4) The <u>Sale and Supply of Goods Act</u> states that products must <u>fit their description</u>, be of <u>satisfactory quality</u> and be <u>fit for purpose</u>.

Products That Meet Safety Standards Are Labelled

1) The <u>British Standards Institution</u> (<u>BSI</u>) produces strict standards on product <u>safety</u> and <u>quality</u>. Companies can have their products <u>tested</u> to see if they <u>meet</u> these <u>standards</u> and <u>Kitemark requirements</u> — if so, they can display the <u>Kitemark symbol</u> on their products. ➡

2) The Lion Mark shows that a toy has been <u>made</u> by a member of the <u>British Toy and Hobby Association</u> who agrees to stick to strict <u>safety</u>, <u>marketing</u> and <u>ethical</u> guidelines.

3) The CE mark is the manufacturer's <u>claim</u> that the product meets the <u>essential safety standards</u>, allowing it to be sold <u>throughout Europe</u>.

It's <u>worthwhile</u> for a company to try to meet safety standards, as it could make their products <u>more profitable</u> — many consumers are more willing to buy 'approved' products, or will <u>pay more</u> for them.

This book — 'NOT SUITABLE FOR CATS, DOGS OR HAMSTERS'

For products to be <u>safe</u>, <u>consumers</u> need to use them for what they are <u>designed for</u> and follow <u>advice</u>.

Safety and Moral Issues

Manufacturers also have a <u>moral</u> and <u>legal</u> responsibility to make sure that their <u>workers</u> have <u>fair working conditions</u> and a <u>safe</u> working environment.

Working Conditions Can Affect People, Costs and Sales

Manufacturers can <u>reduce costs</u> by:

1) Paying workers <u>less money</u>.
2) Increasing staff <u>working hours</u>.
3) Reducing <u>sick pay</u> and <u>holidays</u>.
4) Reducing the amount of money spent on <u>health and safety</u> (see p.70).

<u>BUT</u> if they do this, then:

1) They could <u>lose employees</u> — or employees could go on <u>strike</u>.
2) They could also <u>anger</u> potential <u>customers</u> — who might then choose <u>not</u> to buy the company's products.

None of this would be <u>good for business</u>.

Most countries (e.g. UK) have <u>laws</u> about <u>working practices</u> to <u>protect workers</u> (e.g. laws about minimum pay and maximum number of working hours etc.). However, many textile products are <u>produced</u> in <u>poorer</u> countries with <u>fewer laws</u>. Often <u>child labour</u> and <u>sweatshops</u> (where conditions and pay are terrible) are used to produce textiles <u>cheaply</u>. In many cases the workers <u>can't strike</u> because they'd lose their jobs...

There are Initiatives for Better Working Conditions

Many consumers are <u>concerned</u> about the <u>welfare</u> of people who <u>make</u> the textile products in our shops. They want to buy <u>ethically traded</u> products, which means that the people who make them are <u>not exploited</u> (taken advantage of) — i.e. they work in <u>safe</u> conditions and are paid <u>fairly</u>. People are often willing to <u>pay more</u> to buy ethically traded products. To promote <u>better conditions</u> for workers in <u>developing countries</u> the <u>Ethical Trading Initiative</u> (ETI) was set up:

1) The ETI is a group of <u>companies</u>, <u>trade unions</u> and <u>volunteer groups</u> from all over the world.
2) Companies in the ETI agree to meet <u>standards</u> covering things like <u>wages</u>, <u>working hours</u> and <u>health and safety</u>.
3) The ETI <u>checks</u> that companies are following the rules and gives them <u>advice</u> about how they can improve.

Ethically traded products are often <u>labelled with symbols</u> so that consumers can identify them. <u>Fair trade</u> products are products made in <u>developing countries</u> by <u>farmers</u> and <u>workers</u> who have been paid a <u>fair price</u>.

Practice Questions

1) Suggest a warning that should be put on a <u>toy</u> containing <u>small parts</u> that a young child might <u>choke</u> on.

2) Tom ordered some trousers from a <u>mail order</u> catalogue. When they arrived, they were a <u>different</u> colour from the one described in the catalogue. Which <u>law</u> protects Tom so that he can send these trousers back and get a <u>new pair</u> or a <u>refund</u>?

3) a) What <u>symbol</u> might you see on a product that has been made by a member of the British Toy and Hobby Association?
   b) What does the <u>CE</u> symbol mean?

4) Explain why products made by a <u>less ethical</u> manufacturer might be <u>cheaper to buy</u> than those made by a manufacturer who practises <u>ethical trading</u>.

Environmental Issues

Making, using and disposing of textile products can have a negative impact on the environment...

Fabric Production Pollutes and Uses Up Finite Resources

1) Farming natural fibres (e.g. cotton) often uses artificial fertilisers and pesticides to increase crop yields — these can pollute rivers, harm wildlife and can kill other creatures (not just pests).

2) Synthetic fibres are made from non-renewable resources, e.g. polyester fibres are made from crude oil.

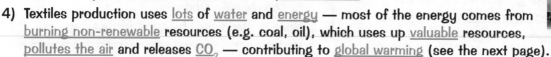

Non-renewable resources are finite — they will run out.

3) Synthetic and regenerated fibres are processed using chemicals (see pages 20-21), some of which are released into waste water that ends up in streams or rivers and can poison wildlife.

4) Textiles production uses lots of water and energy — most of the energy comes from burning non-renewable resources (e.g. coal, oil), which uses up valuable resources, pollutes the air and releases CO_2 — contributing to global warming (see the next page).

5) Dyeing and finishing processes may involve toxic chemicals that can also end up in waste water (see above).

Ways to reduce these impacts include:

1) Reducing the use of fertilisers/pesticides or using environmentally-friendly ones, e.g. natural predators as pesticides.

2) Producing synthetic fibres from recycled resources, e.g. Polartec® fleece from plastic bottles.

3) Reusing chemicals in production processes, e.g. chemicals used to make Tencel® are reused to make more Tencel®.

4) Using energy from renewable resources (e.g. wind power) or reducing/recycling water and energy used.

5) Removing chemicals from the waste water before it leaves factories and disposing of the chemical sludge safely, or using biodegradable (see below) or natural chemicals in the dyeing and finishing processes.

Using Fabric Products Can Harm the Environment

Cleaning textiles products at home or dry-cleaning often involves toxic chemicals (in detergents and solvents), which can pollute waterways. Also, washing textile products at high temperatures uses lots of energy.

These issues can be reduced by using environmentally-friendly cleaning products and by producing textile products that can be washed at lower temperatures.

Throwing Away Old Products Increases Landfill

When textile products and their packaging become redundant (are no longer needed or useful) they're thrown away. The waste usually ends up in landfill sites, and some things can take hundreds of years to decompose (e.g. synthetic fibres). Also, light packaging (e.g. plastics) can be blown off landfill sites and can suffocate wildlife where it ends up.

Products and packaging can be disposed of in a safe and environmentally-friendly way by:

Reusing them — e.g. garments can be taken to charity shops or given to collections for third world countries.
Recycling them — e.g. fabrics can be recycled in three ways (see p.62) and plastic packaging can be recycled too.

The environmental impact can be limited by using less packaging and by making both products and packaging out of biodegradable materials.

Biodegradable materials are broken down naturally (by bacteria).

I have an issue with my environment — it's raining...

In the last few years, consumers have begun to be far more aware of issues like these. As a result, many manufacturers have started to clean up their act and try to reduce their environmental impact.

Environmental Issues

The Use of Some Harmful Chemicals is Being Reduced

Many chemicals used in the textiles industry have been found to be harmful to the environment. Over recent years, there have been efforts to reduce their use:

1) Scouring (cleaning) polyester and knitted fabrics used to involve chemicals called CFCs. When CFCs get into the upper atmosphere they break down the ozone layer. This is bad news because the ozone layer protects the Earth from the Sun's harmful UV radiation. Since the 1980s, countries have been forced by international agreements to reduce their CFC use. Now they're not used at all in textiles production in developed countries.

2) Adding finishes to fabrics can release gases called VOCs. VOCs are air pollutants and some are also greenhouse gases (see below). International agreements (such as the 1991 Geneva Protocol) have made countries agree to reduce their VOC emissions.

3) Whitening fabric before dyeing can be done using chlorine-based bleaches — when these are present in waste water they can poison wildlife. Many textile companies are now using safer oxygen/peroxide-based ones or are producing unbleached fabrics, e.g. unbleached cotton.

Products have a Carbon Footprint

1) A carbon footprint is the amount of greenhouse gases released by doing or making something.

> Greenhouse gases, like carbon dioxide (CO_2), are gases that contribute to the greenhouse effect. They limit how much heat can escape from the Earth's atmosphere — releasing lots of these gases is causing the planet's temperature to rise.

2) All products have a carbon footprint because fossil fuels are burned to provide the energy for making and transporting them, which releases CO_2.

3) So the more energy that's needed to make something, the bigger its carbon footprint.

4) A product's carbon footprint is affected by the distance it travels from where it's made to where it's used (this is called product miles). E.g. lots of textile products that are sold in the UK are made overseas, so they have a high number of product miles.

Carbon Emissions Can Be Offset

Carbon emissions is a general phrase used to describe greenhouse gas emissions.

1) Manufacturers and retailers can choose to have any carbon emissions they make offset — this means donating money to projects that reduce carbon emissions to balance out the greenhouse gases that they're responsible for.

2) Projects include planting trees, investing in wind and solar power, and in recycling projects.

3) Offsetting is often a good marketing tool, because many people prefer to buy products that are more environmentally friendly.

Practice Questions

1) Give two ways in which the textiles industry uses up natural resources.

2) Suggest two ways of reducing the amount of waste from textiles products that goes into landfill.

3) Explain why CFCs are harmful to the environment.

4) a) What is a carbon footprint?
   b) Explain why all products have a carbon footprint.
   c) Suggest one way in which a product's carbon footprint might be reduced.

5) Suggest two ways in which textile businesses can try to offset their carbon emissions.

Sustainability

Making products that are <u>sustainable</u> at each stage of their <u>life cycle reduces</u> the <u>environmental impact</u>.

Sustainable Products <u>are</u> Better for the Environment

Sustainability means not causing <u>permanent damage</u> to the environment and not using up <u>finite resources</u> (ones that'll run out eventually).

How sustainable a product is depends on the <u>materials</u> used (e.g. are they recyclable?), the <u>processes</u> used to make it (e.g. does the energy come from renewable resources?) and the <u>design</u> itself (e.g. is the product designed to last?)

You can use the <u>6 Rs</u> when you're designing, to <u>reduce the impact</u> of your product on the <u>environment</u> and make the whole process more <u>sustainable</u>...

<u>Wood pulp</u> (see p.20) is a <u>renewable</u> resource — trees can be <u>replanted</u>.

EXAM TIP:
Make sure you can apply the 6 Rs to specific products.

Remember to Use the 6 Rs

1) REPAIR

- It's better to <u>mend</u> textile products <u>instead</u> of <u>throwing</u> them away and replacing them as soon as they get damaged.

- This means designing things so they're <u>easy to repair</u> — a <u>simple design</u> sold with <u>spare components</u> (e.g. <u>matching</u> buttons, thread) that can be used to <u>mend</u> the product.

  E.g. when sequins fall off a bag (like this one), they can be replaced if spare sequins are provided with the bag.

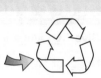

- Manufacturers can also make a <u>profit</u> by selling <u>replacement parts</u> for some textile products, e.g. spare cushions for cushion covers, tent patches, etc.

- <u>Not all</u> textile products <u>can be repaired</u> (e.g. carpets) and sometimes it's <u>not worth</u> repairing them (e.g. knickers, socks) because they're so <u>cheap</u> to buy (due to being <u>mass produced</u>).

2) RECYCLE

- Recycling means <u>reprocessing</u> waste materials so they can be used again. It usually uses <u>less energy</u> and <u>finite resources</u> than obtaining <u>new</u> materials — e.g. fibres can be <u>mechanically extracted</u> (called <u>pulling</u>) from old clothes instead of being made from raw materials.

- Designers can <u>design</u> textile products to be <u>recycled</u> by making them <u>easy</u> to be <u>disassembled</u> (taken apart) into their <u>pre-manufactured components</u> (which can be <u>reused</u>) and <u>fabrics</u>. The <u>fabrics</u> can then recycled in one of <u>three ways</u>:

  1) <u>Primary</u> — fabrics are reprocessed into <u>fibres</u> which are used to make the <u>same products</u>. E.g. a polyester garment can be broken down into polyester fibres which are used in more polyester fabric.

  2) <u>Secondary</u> — fabrics are reprocessed into <u>fibres</u> and used to make <u>different products</u>. E.g. fibres from all sorts of clothing fabrics can be used as furniture/mattress padding or insulation.

  3) <u>Tertiary</u> — fabrics are reprocessed into their <u>basic components</u> and <u>reused</u>. E.g. polyester can be broken down into its basic chemicals (esters) and reused.

- This <u>symbol</u> is found on <u>textile products</u> or <u>packaging</u> that <u>can be recycled</u>. <u>Plastic packaging</u> can be recycled and used to make <u>new plastic products</u>.

I've realised cramming isn't sustainable...

A nice little <u>tip</u> for you here: Section A of your exam focuses on <u>sustainability</u> — which means you're <u>going</u> to get tested on this stuff. So if I were you, I'd make sure I knew these two pages <u>back to front</u>.

Sustainability

3) REUSE

- A <u>product's life</u> can be <u>extended</u> by <u>using it again</u>, e.g. unwanted clothes can be passed on to <u>friends</u> and <u>relatives</u>, <u>charity shops</u> or <u>third world countries</u> to be worn again.
- Some people <u>reuse</u> products for <u>other purposes</u>, e.g. using an <u>old t-shirt</u> as a <u>duster</u>.

  Products can be <u>adapted</u> for another purpose, e.g. trousers could be <u>dyed</u>, <u>decorated</u> and <u>re-fashioned</u> into a bag.

- Some products are <u>designed</u> for reuse, e.g. reusable nappies.
- Reusing a product means you <u>don't</u> have to use up <u>more material</u> and <u>energy</u> making a replacement.

4) RETHINK

Designers need to <u>think differently</u> in order to make a product more sustainable.
They need to:
- <u>Rethink materials</u> — e.g. use materials made from <u>renewable resources</u>, or that are <u>recyclable</u>, <u>recycled</u> or <u>biodegradable</u>.
- <u>Rethink the purpose</u> of the product — e.g. a product could have <u>more than one use</u>, like trousers that can turn into shorts.

5) REDUCE

- Some products have what's known as '<u>built-in obsolescence</u>', which is when manufacturers design their product to <u>need replacing</u> within a few months or years, e.g. <u>cheap, low-quality clothes</u>. Making <u>long-lasting</u>, <u>durable</u> products instead, <u>reduces</u> the <u>number</u> of products customers need to buy. Manufacturers would then be making fewer products and so <u>cutting down</u> on <u>energy</u> use, <u>transport</u> and <u>materials</u>.

- The <u>life cycle</u> of a product is from its <u>design to disposal</u>. It includes the <u>raw materials</u> used to make it, the <u>production processes</u>, <u>transport and distribution</u>, its <u>intended use</u>, <u>care and maintenance</u> of the product, and its <u>disposal</u>.

  The <u>eco-footprint</u> of a product is the <u>amount of land</u> needed to <u>sustain</u> the <u>resources</u> used to <u>make</u> it and to <u>dispose</u> of it <u>safely</u>. It's usually <u>measured</u> in <u>hectares of land</u>. More <u>sustainable products</u> have <u>smaller eco-footprints</u>.

All parts of the <u>life cycle</u> of a product can be <u>changed</u> to <u>reduce</u> its <u>eco-footprint</u>.
For example, <u>reducing emissions</u> or <u>waste materials</u> during the production process, or making transportation of raw materials more <u>energy-efficient</u> will decrease a product's eco-footprint.

6) REFUSE

- You can <u>refuse</u> to buy a product if you think it's <u>bad for the environment</u>, e.g. you could refuse to buy cheap, low-quality clothes that might encourage a <u>throwaway society</u>.
- When you're <u>designing</u> a product you can <u>refuse</u> to <u>use materials</u> that haven't been or can't be <u>recycled</u> or that are <u>harmful</u> to the environment (see 'rethink' above).

Practice Questions

1) What does the term <u>finite resource</u> mean?
2) What is meant by <u>primary recycling</u> of fabrics?
3) Give <u>three</u> ways a t-shirt could be reused.
4) What is meant by <u>built-in obsolescence</u>?
5) Sarah is designing a beaded cushion. With reference to the <u>6 Rs</u> describe <u>two ways</u> in which she could reduce the cushion's impact on the environment.

Production Methods

There are <u>different ways</u> of making textile products, depending on <u>how many</u> you're going to <u>make</u>:

One-off Production *is Making a Single Unique Product*

> <u>One-off production</u> (or "<u>job production</u>") is where an <u>exclusive</u> textile product is made to meet an <u>individual client's specifications</u>, e.g. a custom-made wedding dress.

1) The product is <u>high-quality</u> — it's made by one person or a small team, either by hand or by skilled machinists.
2) Before work is started on the actual product, a <u>prototype</u> (called a <u>toile</u>) is often made from a <u>cheaper</u> material to make sure there are no problems with the design or fit.
3) The product takes a <u>long time</u> to make, and the high labour and material costs (as materials aren't bought in bulk) make it <u>expensive</u>.

Batch Production *is Making a Set Number of Products*

> <u>Batch production</u> is when a <u>specific</u> number of <u>identical products</u>, called a <u>batch</u>, are made to order (e.g. 100 white fedora hats).

1) Machines can be <u>altered</u> so that a different batch can be made — maybe in a different colour, size or style (e.g. 200 straw boaters). This is good because the manufacturer can react to <u>specific orders</u>.
2) <u>Small changes</u> to the product are very <u>easy</u> to make because you <u>don't</u> need to alter the machinery and tools a lot. For example, you only need to change the colour of the thread and fabric if you want to change the colour of the product.
3) The products are made in <u>standard sizes</u> — they can't be tailored to fit individuals like in one-off production.
4) The production is broken down into <u>separate</u> tasks, which are completed one after another. A team of people often work together to do these tasks. Each person usually repeats the same task, so they become <u>skilled</u> which helps to <u>improve</u> the product's <u>consistency</u> and <u>quality</u>.
5) However, staff do have to be <u>flexible</u> and <u>trained</u> to deal with <u>different</u> batches.

"So how is this batch?"
"Bobbin' along nicely."

6) The production <u>costs</u> of batch production are <u>less</u> per item than in one-off production because of <u>economies of scale</u> (see next page).
7) However, batch production has some <u>problems</u> — production <u>time</u> is <u>lost between batches</u> while equipment is being set up differently and <u>nothing's being made</u>.

Mass Production *is Making Large Numbers of Products*

1) <u>Mass production</u> (or "<u>volume production</u>") is used to make a <u>large quantity</u> of identical products. It's used for products that'll be produced for <u>a long time</u> with <u>few design changes</u>, e.g. socks. Products must be designed to be <u>suitable</u> for the process (a <u>simple design</u> in <u>standard sizes</u>).
2) Mass production's <u>expensive</u> to <u>set up</u> initially, but produces lots of identical products for a very <u>low cost</u> per item. Again, this is because of <u>economies of scale</u>...

Der der der der, derder-der der der — it's batch of the day...

One-off, batch and mass production... you need to know <u>what they are</u> and <u>what they're good for</u>.

Production Methods

Economies of Scale Reduce Manufacturing Costs

The cost of an item gets lower the more of it you produce — this is called economy of scale. It means batch-produced products are generally cheaper than one-off products, because:

1) Materials and components (e.g. fastenings) can be bought in bulk which allows manufacturers to negotiate discounts — because they're buying so much.

2) Workers repeat the same task over and over again and can become quicker and more efficient at doing that task.

3) The high cost of machines is spread out over the large number of products that they churn out.

4) High-volume production is often done using computer-controlled machines. Using CAD/CAM makes production more efficient (see p.43), so it reduces manufacturing costs.

Just In Time Can Make Production More Efficient

In a Just In Time (JIT) system, a manufacturer gets the materials and components delivered frequently in small amounts and uses them as soon as they're delivered. This process can be automated using ICT — computer systems automatically order more materials and components when they're needed.

The advantages of Just In Time production are:

1) It saves on the cost of storing materials, and means there's less money tied-up in stock.

2) It avoids money being wasted through stock going out of date, or unsold finished products piling up.

BUT, materials and components must be delivered on time and fault free — there's no time to return poor quality materials or wait for late deliveries.

Choosing the Right Production Method is Important

When you're choosing the production method for a textiles product, think about the target market. Will they pay lots of money for a one-off item? Or will they want a low-cost, mass-produced item?

Haute Couture describes one-off fashion design, usually by a designer fashion house (e.g. Christian Dior or Givenchy).

Designers use the highest quality fabrics and detailed designs or decoration which can be very expensive. Only a small number of very wealthy people can afford these designs.

"Off-the-peg" clothes are bought ready-to-wear from a shop. These items are cheaper because they're mass-produced. Designers need to think about the costs of materials, use more straightforward designs and design products in standard sizes.

Practice Questions

1) List two reasons why one-off production is expensive.
2) Explain what batch production is.
3) Why can batch production be inefficient?
4) A factory batch produces different coloured t-shirts. Explain why batch production is a good production method for making t-shirts.
5) Describe what is meant by economy of scale.
6) Explain why people may be prepared to pay more to have their clothes manufactured using one-off production.

Quality Control

It's important that products are of a <u>satisfactory quality</u> — otherwise nobody will buy them.

Good Design and Good Manufacture are Different

A well-designed product:
- can carry out its <u>function</u> really well
- <u>looks</u> good and attracts consumers

A well-manufactured product:
- has been <u>made</u> to a <u>good standard</u> — things like the finish, seams, colour and material are all satisfactory
- is <u>accurate</u> to the original design

Quality is Affected by Materials and Processes

The quality of your finished product will be affected by the <u>design choices</u> you make about:

1) The <u>materials</u>, e.g. denim would be a good choice for trousers because it's hard wearing and good for everyday use. (Silk would be nice too but probably wouldn't last very long if you tried to wear the trousers for general use everyday.)

2) The <u>processes</u>, e.g. using a French seam on baby clothes so there aren't any rough edges to irritate the skin. (Other types of seam would be able to hold the clothes together but wouldn't be as comfortable for the baby to wear.)

Accuracy is Important When Making a Product

To make a <u>high quality</u> product you need to be <u>accurate</u>.

1) Whether you're making a one-off item or a whole batch, you need to be <u>precise</u> when you're cutting around a pattern so that all the parts fit together correctly.

2) If you're producing <u>lots</u> of the same item you need to make sure they're all consistent. <u>Templates</u> can help with this — e.g. you could make a template to make it easy to position the buttons or pockets correctly.

"So all I have to do is cut along the dotted lines?"

3) It's hard to get things absolutely perfect even if you do use a template, so there'll be a <u>small</u> amount of error that's <u>allowed</u> — this is the <u>tolerance</u> (see the next page).

4) Using <u>CAD/CAM</u> (see page 42-43) helps with accuracy. For example, a CAM machine will cut out fabric accurately every time.

Quality Control Checks The Quality of Manufacture

1) To make sure products are manufactured to a high quality, <u>quality control checks</u> need to be included throughout the manufacturing process.

2) Quality control means <u>testing samples</u> of the product and materials, at various stages, to check that they meet specifications (see next page). For example, buttons must be attached securely and hems must be straight.

I can assure you that this page is quality...

A <u>high quality</u> product is one that <u>does its job</u> well, looks good, is manufactured <u>consistently</u> and is <u>accurate</u> to the original design. If it does all that, it ought to <u>keep customers happy</u> too.

Quality Control

Quality is Checked at Critical Points

Quality control checks happen at three main critical control points during production. These checks are made on:

Raw Materials

Raw materials are checked to make sure that the right order has been delivered from the supplier, and that the materials are in good condition and match the production plan.

Prototype

A final prototype (or sample) product will be manufactured to check that the production plan is exactly right. This prototype will also be compared to the design specification to check that all the design criteria have been met. Any problems identified when making the prototype will need to be solved, and the production plan modified to include the changes.

Production Samples

The production plan will specify several points in the production process where quality should be checked. At these points, a sample product is taken and checked (either visually or using a computer) to make sure it's correct. If there is a fault then modifications need to be made.

Samples of the completed product will be checked too.

Here's an example of a flow chart showing the stages of production for a shirt. The quality control points are shown in diamond-shaped boxes.

```
        Start
          │
  Cut out fabric pieces ◄──── no
          │
  Are pieces the
  correct sizes? ──── yes
          │
  Join front and
  back pieces
          │
  Sew buttonholes
          │
  Attach sleeves
  and collar
          │
  Attach pocket
  to shirt ◄────
          │
  Is pocket on
  straight? ──── no
          │ yes
  Attach buttons
          │
  Is the final ──── no
  product ok?
          │ yes
        Finish
```

Tolerances are the Margins of Error

When quality checks on parts of a product are being carried out, the manufacturer will allow measurements to be within certain tolerances.

The gap between these two limits is the tolerance of the hem.

10 mm | 8 mm

Tolerance in testing is given as an upper (+) and lower (−) limit for the measurement. For example, if a hem should have a width of 9 mm (± 1) then a measurement of 8 mm for the hem would be OK, but 11 mm would not. Tolerances are usually given in the production plan.

Practice Questions

1) Give two characteristics of
   a) a well-designed product
   b) a well-manufactured product.

2) Quality can be affected by materials and the processes used to make the item. Give an example of how each can affect the quality of an item of baby clothing.

3) A piece of fabric that should measure 105 mm in length could actually be up to 5 mm longer or shorter. How would this tolerance be written in the production plan?

4) Explain why accuracy is important during the production of a textile product.

5) Explain how quality control checks are used to ensure the quality of a product.

Labelling

Textile products have <u>labels</u> and <u>tags</u> that give all sorts of <u>information</u>, e.g. fibre content, care instructions, designer and size. Some of this information is shown as <u>symbols</u> and you need to know what they mean.

Textile Products Must Have *Fabric Care Labels*

1) A <u>care label</u> is a fabric label stitched onto a product. It includes the following information...

- <u>Fibre content</u> (compulsory)
- <u>Care symbols</u>
- <u>Extra</u> care instructions
- (The <u>size</u> might be shown too)

100% PURE SILK

HAND OR MACHINE
WASH SEPARATELY

EXTRA LARGE

The 'red sock left in
wash look' didn't help
Reg at Wimbledon.

2) <u>Extra information</u> about a product might also be shown, either on the care label or on a separate label. E.g. <u>quality</u> marks.

PURE NEW WOOL

Care Labels *Tell You How to Look After the Product*

An <u>International Textile Care Labelling Code</u> has been developed with <u>symbols</u> to tell people <u>how to care</u> for their textile products.

Here are some of the symbols you can find on care labels...

The symbols are also found on washing machine dials and on washing powder packaging.

WASHING INSTRUCTIONS

When you're washing a fabric you need to think about four things:

1) <u>Temperature</u> — <u>High temperatures</u> can help <u>remove stains</u> but can also cause some fabrics to <u>change shape</u>.
2) <u>Action</u> — <u>Vigorous</u> washing can help remove stains too but might <u>damage</u> more delicate fabrics.
3) <u>Time</u> — Some fabrics can <u>stain</u> if they're left in water too long. They often need <u>hand washing</u>.
4) <u>Detergent</u> — Strong <u>detergents</u> (soaps) can get things <u>very clean</u> but might <u>damage</u> some fabrics, e.g. silk, or cause dyes to come out of the fabric so the <u>colour changes</u>.

40º	Maximum temperature 40º
30º	Maximum temperature 30º Mild process
	Hand wash only
	Do not bleach
	Do not wash

DRYING INSTRUCTIONS

○	Tumble dry beneficial
	Do not tumble dry

Most things can be dried on the <u>washing line</u>. But some garments (e.g. <u>knitted</u> clothes) can become <u>stretched</u>, so they need to be <u>laid flat</u> instead. <u>Tumble drying</u> is good for getting clothes dry but can cause some fabrics (e.g. <u>wool</u> and <u>polyester</u>) to <u>shrink</u>.

IRONING INSTRUCTIONS

⌐	Cool iron
⌐⌐	Warm iron
⌐⌐⌐	Hot iron
	Do not iron

Ironing <u>removes creases</u>. You need to use the <u>right temperature</u> — <u>too hot</u> and you could <u>melt</u>, <u>burn</u> or <u>shrink</u> the fabric. The <u>dots</u> in the iron symbol tell you how <u>hot</u> you should have the iron.

DRY CLEANING INSTRUCTIONS

Ⓐ	Dry clean in all solvents
	Do not dry clean

Some fabrics might change shape if they <u>absorb</u> a lot of <u>moisture</u>. So you should have them <u>dry cleaned</u>. This means using <u>chemicals</u> (solvents) to clean them instead of water.

I found this under my armpit:

When you leave home and have to do all your own <u>washing</u>, you'll be glad that you studied this page. <u>Shrinking</u> your pricey pure lamb's wool sweater to the size of a doll's jumper isn't really funny.

Labelling

New Technologies Make Printing Labels Easy

New technology has made it easy to print high quality fabric labels.

These labelling methods are sometimes called smart labelling.

1) Thermal printing lets you use print on both sides of a fabric label in a range of colours — meaning you can have loads of jazzy styles of label.

2) It also allows you to print on different types of fabric, e.g. satin, nylon or polyester.

3) Ultrasonic cutting machines are often used to cut the labels — they produce a very smooth cut so the edge of the label isn't scratchy.

4) These technologies mean you can print different types of label 'in house' without having to order them in, e.g. sew-in labels with things like care information on, swing tickets (the ones that dangle from a product until you cut them off) or adhesive labels. A fancy label can make a product more desirable, e.g. a laser cut embossed label suggests a luxury product.

Tagging Textiles Helps Manufacturers Too

Labels and tags are useful for manufacturers and retailers as well as for consumers.

Stock checking is an important task that needs to be done on a regular basis — it's important for companies to keep track of what they've got so they don't order excess stock or can order more before they run out.

BARCODES

1) Barcodes are a simple and common way of labelling all sorts of items.

2) The barcode can be used to identify exactly what the item is, who made it and how much the item costs.

3) Each time an item is sold, the barcode is scanned and the sale recorded. This means you can monitor stock levels in a shop by checking the number of items sold against the number that were delivered.

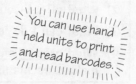

You can use hand held units to print and read barcodes.

RADIO FREQUENCY IDENTIFICATION (RFID)

1) RFID labels contain a small computer chip which, like a barcode, stores information about the product. The information can be read by a special receiver which communicates with the chip using radio waves.

RFID labels are sometimes called smart labels too.

2) The information stored on the chip can be updated, meaning the tags can be reused, which is more environmentally friendly and cost effective.

3) Tags can be read from further away than barcodes and you can read more than one tag at once — so the moment the product arrives in the shop or warehouse the stock control system is updated. This makes stock checking faster and more accurate.

4) RFID labels can also monitor exactly where a particular item is in a warehouse or shop.

5) But the downside is, RFID labels are much more expensive to produce than barcodes.

Practice Questions

1) What information is it compulsory to show on a garment's care label?

2) Give one advantage and one disadvantage of washing clothes at a high temperature.

3) How should knitted garments be dried? Why is this?

4) Describe what RFID labels are and explain how they can make stock checking easier.

Section Five — Industrial Awareness

Health and Safety

Health and safety is essential for people working in textiles production — you don't want to find a finger sewn onto your new hat. So manufacturers need to carry out risk assessments...

Employers Must Complete a "Risk Assessment"...

1) The Health and Safety at Work Act says that businesses must complete a risk assessment for each stage of production.

2) The risk assessment identifies what must be done for the work area to be safe for employees.

3) The results of the assessment have to be checked by a Health and Safety Inspector.

> **The risk assessment looks at:**
> 1) Using tools and equipment.
> 2) Using materials and chemicals.
> 3) Correct protective clothing.
> 4) Safe working practices.

...To Identify and Minimise Risks

When performing a risk assessment you need to first identify any potential risks or hazards, and then put precautions in place to minimise the risk, e.g. placing warning or caution signs on machines, or erecting barriers and guards.

When you're writing a risk assessment think:

1) What could go wrong?
2) What effect would this have?
3) What can I do to prevent it happening?
4) What precautions could I take to make sure the risk is minimised?

Consider the manufacture of a denim bag:

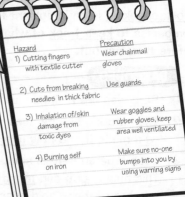

Hazard	Precaution
1) Cutting fingers with textile cutter	Wear chainmail gloves
2) Cuts from breaking needles in thick fabric	Use guards
3) Inhalation of/skin damage from toxic dyes	Wear goggles and rubber gloves, keep area well ventilated
4) Burning self on iron	Make sure no-one bumps into you by using warning signs

Accidents Need to be Reported

1) No matter how careful you are, accidents can still happen. All accidents and injuries need to be reported, no matter how minor they are.

2) It's important that workplaces have a clear accident procedure (a set of instructions) so that people know what to do if there's an accident, and how the accident should be reported.

3) The accident procedure should be clearly displayed and cover things like:

- Where the nearest emergency exits and assembly points are.
- Who the first aiders are.
- Where the medical room is.
- Who the accident should be reported to.

1) In a school classroom, you should report all accidents to your teacher straight away. In industry, accidents are recorded on an incident report form and kept in a file.

2) Most companies have a health and safety officer who will investigate each accident to find out what caused it and to see if anything can be done to reduce the risk of the same accident happening again.

Health and safety stopped me putting a gag on this page...

Health and safety might seem like a faff but it's there to try and stop accidents from happening. Make sure you know how manufacturers perform risk assessments and what to do if there's an accident.

Health and Safety

Here are the four main areas of a risk assessment — and the safety precautions that go with each. Enjoy.

1 Tools and Equipment

Industrial sewing machines and cutting machines should be fitted with...

1) GUARDS to minimise the risk of stitching fingers, eye injuries caused by broken needles, etc.

2) DUST EXTRACTORS — to minimise inhalation of textile dust. They should be used with adequate ventilation.

3) Visible EMERGENCY STOP buttons in case of electrocution or accidents.

When working with scissors, craft knives and other sharp objects...

1) Take care when cutting, and use non slip mats and steel safety rulers with craft knives.

2) Avoid injury when carrying blades by pointing the blade downwards from your body and attaching blade covers on knives.

3) Wear a thimble when using pins and needles and store all sharp objects safely.

2 Materials and Chemicals

1) Most chemicals will have COSHH (Control of Substances Hazardous to Health) guidelines and regulations — these will tell you:
   - what hazards the chemical presents
   - how to use, store, then dispose of the chemical safely
   - what protective equipment to wear

2) For example, when using toxic chemicals such as dyes and finishes, you need adequate ventilation and fume extraction to avoid inhalation of vapours. You also need protective clothing to protect the skin and eyes from splashes and spillages.

3) Correct disposal of chemicals is important to protect the environment. E.g. some dyes can be diluted and washed away, but others might need to be collected by an authorised contractor.

EXAM TIP
Make sure you read carefully whether the question's asking for safety measures employers or employees should take.

3 Protective Clothing

1) When using cutting machines wear chain mail gloves to protect your hands.

2) When using chemicals wear rubber gloves and goggles.

3) When sewing wear a hair net or tie long hair back to stop it from getting caught in the machine.

4) Workers using noisy machinery for a long time must wear ear protection.

4 Working Practices

1) The layout of the room should be designed with safety in mind. There must be enough space around each machine. Walkways and exits must always be kept clear, and workspaces should be kept tidy — e.g. chemicals should be put away after use.

2) There must be enough light — if possible it should be natural light.

3) Employees should take regular breaks so they don't get tired and lose concentration.

4) Machinery should be well maintained and checked regularly and safety notices should be clearly displayed.

Practice Questions

1) What is the purpose of a risk assessment?

2) What four areas of manufacturing textiles does the risk assessment need to cover?

3) Terry is going to tie dye his T-shirt using a chemical dye that is toxic. Suggest some precautions he should take.

4) Write a risk assessment for using an industrial sewing machine.

Exam Technique

1) There is <u>one</u> textiles paper called '<u>Sustainability and technical aspects of designing and making</u>'.
2) This paper is about <u>all</u> the things you have learnt during the course.
   It's worth <u>80 marks</u> and lasts <u>1 hr 30 mins</u>.

The Textiles Paper Has *Two Parts...*

...Section A *begins with 15 Short Answer* Questions...

This'll contain <u>multiple choice</u> questions, <u>true and false</u> questions and some questions where you have to <u>write</u> a few words.

> The short questions are worth <u>15</u> out of the 80 marks on the paper.

1 The abbreviation **ETI** stands for:
  (a) Equality Trading Incorporated
  (b) Ethical Training Institute
  (c) Environmental Trading Initiative
  (d) Ethical Trading Initiative [1]

> Read <u>all</u> the answers — don't just go for the first one that sounds possible.

2 What name is given to a design which fits the user well and so won't cause health problems?
  ergonomic [1]

> If you <u>don't know</u> the answer to a multiple choice, you might as well <u>guess</u>. You won't lose a mark, and you might get lucky.

Decide whether this statement is **true** or **false**.

3 Sometimes products are deliberately designed to become obsolete quickly.   True ☑ False ☐ [1]

> Make sure you've learned all the terms in the <u>glossary</u>.

> Don't spend more than <u>a minute</u> on each of these questions — there's only <u>1 mark</u> for each.

...then *Question 16, which is longer*

You'll have to write <u>longer answers</u> for this question. And you might have to do some <u>sketching</u> too...

4 Figure 1 shows a children's outdoor sports jacket. **Fig. 1**
a Identify five specification points for the jacket.

> Question 16 is worth a total of <u>20 marks</u>.

1. It should be made from a material that's easy to clean.
2. It should be made from water resistant material.
3. It should have a comfy, soft inner lining (e.g. brushed cotton).
4. It should be attractive to children, e.g. be made from brightly coloured material.
5. It should be ergonomically designed, e.g. the fastenings should be easy for a child to undo. [5]

> Think about <u>why</u> the product is being manufactured — e.g. it needs to be able to withstand different weather conditions.

> Think about what the <u>consumers</u> want from the product. Here, the <u>target market</u> is <u>children</u> (and <u>parents</u>).

> Try to use <u>technical words</u> such as 'ergonomically' — examiners like to see them.

Exam Technique

b Using notes and sketches, show two examples of how environmental issues could be considered in the design and manufacture of the coat.

Example 1

Fastenings could be made of recycled plastic to reduce waste.

Replacement buttons could be included, so the jacket can be repaired rather than replaced if some of the buttons fall off.

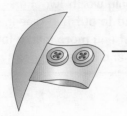

The extra buttons could be sewn onto the inside of the jacket (e.g. on a label) so that they don't need to be put in a plastic bag, which isn't biodegradable.

[3]

Example 2

The jacket could be made from fabrics which can be washed at 30°C. This is better for the environment as washing the jacket will require less energy to heat the water.

The fabric used could also be recyclable, so it doesn't have to be disposed of in a landfill site when the garment is no longer wearable.

This information could be displayed on the jacket using a label containing the following symbols:

low washing temperature — 30°C recyclable symbol

[3]

c Identify a textile product that could be reused and explain how this could be carried out.

A woollen jumper could be reused by giving it to someone

else to wear, or to a charity shop. Or it could be turned

into a different product, e.g. a cushion cover.

[3]

Include as much <u>detail</u> in your notes as possible, even if you think you're <u>stating the obvious</u>.

To get full marks you need to <u>annotate</u> your sketches to explain your ideas. Be as <u>creative</u> as you can.

Make sure you <u>explain</u> how the environmental issues are addressed.

Remember, Section A has a focus on <u>sustainability</u> — so you can bet your last pair of clean undies that there will be loads of questions on <u>environmental issues</u>. Make sure you brush up on the 6 Rs on pages 62-63.

The <u>number of lines</u> you're given for your answer is a big clue to <u>how much</u> you should write (as well as the number of <u>marks</u>).

When you think you've <u>finished</u>, go back and <u>read over</u> your answers to check for <u>mistakes</u>. You might even think of something else you could <u>add</u>.

Exam Technique

And Now For Section B...

Section B focuses on <u>designing</u> products, as well as the <u>technical</u> bits of the course — like working with <u>tools</u> and <u>equipment</u>. It may involve some <u>sketching</u>, as well as writing both <u>short</u> and <u>long</u> answers.

You might be asked about the <u>materials</u> and <u>processes</u> used to design or create a product.

---

17 Figure 2 shows a swimming costume made from a polyester/LYCRA® blend. **Fig. 2**

a Suggest two reasons why this is a suitable fabric for a swimming costume.

It's very stretchy, so it can fit tightly and won't sag

when wet. It also dries quickly so it's easy to wash.

[2]

> There may be more than two reasons why the fabric is suitable — but the question is only worth <u>two marks</u> so you only need to put <u>two reasons</u>. You won't get any more marks for writing more and it just <u>wastes time</u>.

b The swimming costume is made using mass production.

Explain one advantage and one disadvantage of mass production.

Advantage *Products can be made at a lower cost per item because of economies of scale.*

Disadvantage *Designs can't be tailored to meet individual customers' needs — the machines are set up to produce large quantities of standard sizes.*

[4]

> To get <u>all 4 marks</u> you need to <u>explain</u> the reasons.

c *Discuss how a manufacturer might use CAD/CAM to help produce large numbers of the swimming costume.

CAD can be used to design the swimsuit, produce and grade the pattern and create a lay plan. CAM machines use CAD instructions to complete processes like cutting out fabric and producing logos automatically. Computer controlled machines are much quicker and more accurate than machines controlled by people.

[5]

> The asterisk (*) means you can get extra marks for <u>good written communication</u> in this question.
> So check your <u>spelling</u> and use good English. And think about what you want to say <u>before</u> you start writing so you can put your points in a sensible order.

Exam Technique

One of the questions in Section B is likely to ask you to <u>design</u> something to fit a <u>specification</u>.

---

18 'Freshways' supermarket has asked you to design a reusable shopping bag that customers can buy instead of using plastic bags.

The specification for the product is to:
* be environmentally friendly to produce;
* be big enough to hold at least as much shopping as a normal plastic carrier bag;
* display the supermarket's logo on the side — **freshways**

a   Use sketches and notes to show your initial ideas.

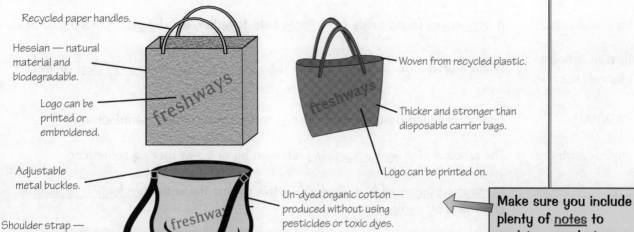

Recycled paper handles.

Hessian — natural material and biodegradable.

Logo can be printed or embroidered.

Adjustable metal buckles.

Shoulder strap — makes bag easier to carry when heavy.

Woven from recycled plastic.

Thicker and stronger than disposable carrier bags.

Logo can be printed on.

Un-dyed organic cotton — produced without using pesticides or toxic dyes.

> Make sure you include plenty of <u>notes</u> to <u>explain</u> your designs.

[4]

b   Use sketches and notes to show your final design idea.
Use annotations to show the design and construction details.

> Make sure you use a <u>sharp pencil</u> (not pen) when you're sketching.

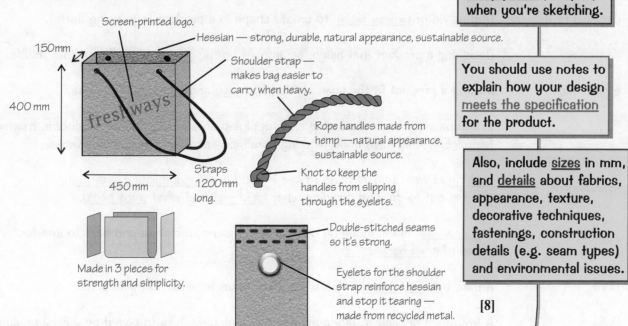

Screen-printed logo.

150mm

400 mm

450 mm

Hessian — strong, durable, natural appearance, sustainable source.

Shoulder strap — makes bag easier to carry when heavy.

Rope handles made from hemp —natural appearance, sustainable source.

Knot to keep the handles from slipping through the eyelets.

Straps 1200mm long.

Made in 3 pieces for strength and simplicity.

Double-stitched seams so it's strong.

Eyelets for the shoulder strap reinforce hessian and stop it tearing — made from recycled metal.

> You should use notes to explain how your design <u>meets the specification</u> for the product.

> Also, include <u>sizes</u> in mm, and <u>details</u> about fabrics, appearance, texture, decorative techniques, fastenings, construction details (e.g. seam types) and environmental issues.

[8]

Glossary

aesthetics	The appearance of an object, for example its colour, shape and texture.
anthropometrics	The study of body measurement data.
appliqué	A decoration made by cutting shapes out of fabric and attaching them on top of another piece of fabric.
biodegradable	Something that can be broken down by bacteria and other organisms.
blended yarn	A yarn made by combining two or more types of fibre.
bonded fabric	A non-woven fabric made from fibres held together, e.g. by glue, stitching or heat.
built-in obsolescence	When a product is designed so that it becomes useless and out of date quickly.
CAD/CAM	Computer-Aided Design linked directly to Computer-Aided Manufacture.
carbon footprint	The amount of greenhouse gases released by doing or making something.
CIM	Computer Integrated Manufacture — this means the entire production process is controlled by computer.
components	Pre-manufactured parts that are added to fabrics to make textile products, e.g. zips.
design specification	A list of characteristics that a product should have.
disassembly	Taking something to pieces to see how it was put together.
disposal of fullness	Getting rid of excess fabric to create shape in a product (e.g. using darts).
eco-design	Designing a product that has a low impact on the environment throughout its life.
ergonomics	Making a product fit the user, so that it's easy and comfortable to use.
ethical trading	Everyone involved in producing and supplying an ethically traded product is treated fairly. E.g. they have good working conditions and get a reasonable wage.
evaluation	Looking at what you've done to see if you have accomplished everything you set out to do, and deciding what went well and what went badly.
felt	A non-woven fabric made by combining pressure, moisture and heat to interlock a mat of wool fibres.
fibre	A thin, hair-like strand. Fibres are often spun together to make yarn.
finish	A treatment applied to fabric at the end of manufacture to give it beneficial qualities.
finite resource	One that will eventually run out.
function	How a product will be used.

Glossary

globalisation	The process of countries becoming more integrated, e.g. textiles products may be made in one country and sold in another.
interfacing	A layer of fabric hidden inside a textile product to give strength, stability or support to an area, e.g. in collars or around buttonholes.
knitted fabric	A fabric made from yarns held together by interlocking loops.
lamination	Sticking together layers of fabric in order to produce a fabric with better properties.
lay plan	The layout of pattern pieces. It should be designed to waste the minimum amount of fabric possible.
manufactured fibres	Fibres that are entirely man-made, e.g. nylon. They're also known as synthetic.
micro-encapsulation	The process of embedding small amounts of chemicals in a fabric to give the fabric beneficial qualities.
microfibres	Really thin synthetic fibres, up to 100 times thinner than a human hair.
mixed fabric	A fabric that has been made using more than one type of yarn.
nanotechnology	This involves tinkering with substances on a really small scale.
overlocker	A type of sewing machine that trims the fabric edge and encases it in thread.
polymer	A long chain of small molecules joined end-to-end, used to make manufactured fibres.
prototype	Full scale model of a design used for final testing before going into production.
quality control	Checks that are carried out on materials and products before, during and after production to make sure that standards are being met.
regenerated fibres	Made from natural materials, which are treated with chemicals to produce fibres.
risk assessment	Identifying the potential hazards at each stage of production and the precautions which need to be taken to minimise risks.
smart material	A material that changes its properties in response to a change in the environment.
sustainable	A sustainable process or material is one that can be used without causing permanent damage to the environment or using up finite resources.
tolerance	The margin of error allowed for a measurement of part of a product. Tolerances are usually given as an upper and lower limit, e.g. 23 mm ($\pm$ 2).
woven fabric	A fabric made by interlacing two sets of yarns together.
yarn	A thread made by twisting fibres together.

Answers

Page 5 — Design Issues

1) a) Wearing a nice piece of clothing (e.g. a nice evening dress / shirt / shoes) can improve a person's self confidence. (Other answers possible.)
   b) E.g. a waterproof jacket / ski jacket will help keep a person warm and dry. (Other answers possible.)

2) Changing styles, technological advances, environmental pressures, taste.

3) It's designing a product that has a low impact on the environment throughout its life.

4) a) Three from, e.g: production costs for companies are lower / better prices for customers / greater product choice for consumers / manufacturers can increase their sales by selling products overseas.
   b) Three from, e.g: more energy is used due to increased transportation / more pollution created due to increased transportation / designers have to take into account the needs of many different cultures, making designing more complicated / some people feel that products from different cultures are becoming more similar and individuality is being lost / in some countries workers are exploited because of poor working conditions in factories.

Page 7 — Product Analysis

1) a) It will give her ideas about — two from, e.g: suitable designs / materials / manufacturing techniques / how to make her product suitable for the target market.
   b) Three from, e.g. components / materials / shape / decoration / price / construction / fitness for purpose.
   c) By taking the hats apart she can find out how the parts were put together and what order they were put together in. It will also show her how any decoration was added to the hats.

2) a) How well a product performs the function it is meant to do.
   b) E.g. by wearing it in heavy rain.
   c) The materials/processes.

Page 9 — Task Analysis and Research

1) a) It's a statement for the designer describing the initial task.
      Three from, e.g: an outline of the background to the task / who the target group is / what kind of product is needed and why / how the product will be used.
   b) It must meet the design brief in terms of function and aesthetics.

2) E.g. they could use a database to keep track of details about products, word processing software to write questionnaires for research and spreadsheets to organise data from the questionnaires.

3) a) parents of babies
   b) Three from, e.g.: do they like a particular style / how much are they willing to pay / where do they buy them from / is there something they'd like that doesn't already exist?

4) a) Yes, Peter is right. Jordan is using closed questions, with no follow-up, so a questionnaire will quickly get her clear results that are easy to analyse.
   b) She'll get more ideas and more detailed information about the sort of beach shoes people want. However, collecting the information might be quite time-consuming and she could end up with information about lots of different types of shoes, which could be hard to analyse.

Page 11 — Design Specification and Proposals

1) Summarise the results, explain the impact of the research on your designs and then suggest ways to move forward.

2) Five from, e.g: aesthetics / safety / fabrics / function / theme / components / financial constraints / target market / construction and decorative techniques.

3) A mood board is lots of different images, words, fabrics, etc. that might trigger ideas for a design.

4) Five from, e.g: the fabric should be absorbent / quick drying / easily washable / hard wearing / it should measure 40-50 x 60-70 cm / it should show the CGP logo / RRP should be 50p or less / it should have funny pictures and bad jokes on it.

5) a) Working from existing products is a good start here, because you need to make something with the same basic structure, but with a few modifications.
   b) A mood board would be useful here, because the basic forms of the covers are established, but the decoration and style can be inspired by a range of Art Deco images.

Page 13 — Generating Design Ideas

1) Four from, e.g: the sketches are drawn and coloured roughly, so they're not very clear / the labels aren't sufficient to explain fully the features of the product / the two ideas are very similar / the products look like they would be impractical to make.

2) Two from, e.g: to produce mood boards / to produce design ideas / to design logos, prints and decorative patterns / to model design ideas in 2D or 3D / to create scaled working drawings, etc.

3) CAD works out the most economical lay plan and automatically calculates the grading.

Page 15 — Design and Development

1) Ergonomics is making products to fit the users. To design things ergonomically you need to use anthropometric data.

2) a) standard dress sizes
   b) three month intervals up to 12 months.
   c) one or two year intervals
   d) collar size
   e) waist size

3) You need to make sure that the cost of your components is in keeping with the intended selling price of your product.

Answers

Page 17 — Development

1) The design specification.

2) To work out the finer details of part of your design and identify any problems.

3) A prototype is a full-scale model of a product.

4) Three from, e.g: to test the size, shape etc. of the design / to make improvements to the design / to avoid wasting time and resources / to test manufacturing processes / to work out the amount of fabric and components needed for production / to plan the equipment and labour required for production / to calculate costings, etc.

5) a) To see if it's fit for purpose, if it's appealing to the target market and if they would consider buying it.
   b) The client, to check it's what they wanted.
   Experts in the textiles industry, to see if they have any suggestions for improvements.

6) Make a model with different fastenings to see if they look better.

Page 19 — Planning

1) a) A detailed plan that tells the manufacturer exactly how to make a product.
   b) Materials needed, measurements and tolerances, lay plans, tools and equipment needed, construction techniques,
   health and safety information, time schedules and quality control instructions.

2) To plan the sequence of tasks to be carried out.

3) A Gantt chart.

Page 21 — Types of Fibre

1) filaments

2) Staple fibres. The yarn looks hairy, rather than smooth, which suggests it's made from lots of short fibres.

3) They come from renewable sources, and the fibres are biodegradable and often recyclable.

4) Wool fibres are harvested from the fleece of a sheep or other animal. The fibres are cleaned and straightened, and then spun into a yarn.

5) Chemically treated cellulose

6) E.g. they're resistant to biological damage and can be heated and set into creases, like pleats. (There are lots of other possible answers.)

7) Microfibres are very expensive. His shorts would cost a lot to make, and so would have to be sold at a high price.

Page 23 — Fabric Construction

1) a) right to left
   b) up and down

2) a) twill
   b) Jacquard
   c) satin
   d) plain

3) E.g. easily crushed, sheds the pile, directional so pattern lay plans need to be carefully designed.

4) warp-knitted fabric

Page 25 — Fibres and Fabrics

1) a) cotton
   b) E.g. wool (cotton or some synthetic fibres can also be used).
   c) E.g. silk (cotton or polyester can also be used).

2) a) Positive: two from, e.g: strong / hard-wearing / absorbent / comfortable / cool in hot weather / easy to wash / easy to add colour to / doesn't cause allergies.
   Negative: two from, e.g. creases easily / highly flammable / poor elasticity / can shrink when washed / dries slowly / dissolved by acids / susceptible to moth and mildew damage.
   b) Positive: two from, e.g: can be strong / warm / absorbent / good elasticity / low flammability / crease resistant.
   Negative: two from, e.g. can shrink when washed / dries slowly / can feel itchy / pilling occurs with abrasion / susceptible to moth and mildew damage.

3) Positive: e.g. resistant to abrasion / strong / extremely elastic / easily washable / resists most chemical and biological damage.
   Negative: e.g. not absorbent / highly flammable / dissolved by chlorine bleach.

4) E.g. it has low flammability, which is an important safety feature in night clothes / it has good elasticity, which helps make clothes comfortable.

5) The polyester shirt. Cotton is highly susceptible to mildew damage, but polyester isn't.

6) a) E.g. linen
   b) E.g. it creases easily. (There are lots of other possible answers.)

7) E.g. can shrink when washed, viscose would be a better fabric to use. (There are lots of other possible answers.)

Page 27 — Fabric Combinations

1) Any four from, e.g: change appearance / create interesting texture effects / improve practical qualities / improve working qualities / make fabric cheaper to produce.

2) elastane

3) Blending — different fibres are spun together to make a yarn. Mixing — different yarns are used together to make a fabric.

4) Three from, e.g: the fabric is stronger / less absorbent, so dries more quickly / is less likely to crease / is less likely to shrink.

5) E.g. to make it waterproof, to make it wipe-clean.

6) Two or more different fabrics are layered and bonded together.

Answers

Page 29 — Smart and Modern Materials

1) a) Nomex®
   b) Neoprene
   c) KEVLAR®

2) E.g. to perfume underwear, to make clothes insect-repelling, in thermochromic fabrics.

3) A fabric that reacts automatically to changes in its surroundings.

4) It can be coated with nanoparticles.

5) E.g. heat-generating fibres to help keep the climber warm, a moisture management system to help keep the climber dry.

Page 31 — Nanotechnology

1) A really really tiny bit of material.

2) a) Nanoparticles prevent dirt sticking to fibres in a fabric and prevent the fibres from absorbing moisture, so the dirt is easy to clean off.
   b) E.g. fire-resistance, chemical-resistance.

3) They don't change the feel/wearability of the fabric.

4) Really thin tubes of carbon.

5) E.g. they conduct heat and electrical signals.

6) They are made from proteins that encourage blood to clot in wounds.

7) Two from, e.g: it's really strong / lightweight / flexible.

Page 33 — Choosing Fabrics

1) a) E.g. mildew resistant, quick drying.
   b) plain or twill for strength

2) a) Any synthetic fabric (e.g. polyester) for mildew resistance.
   b) Any synthetic fabric (e.g. nylon) for resistance to bleach and acidic/alkaline cleaning chemicals.
   c) E.g. organic cotton.

3) a) It has good lustre and drapes well.
   b) Silk is very expensive.

Page 35 — Dyeing and Printing

1) E.g. colours can be changed quickly to respond to fashions.

2) The dye includes a bleaching agent that removes the dark colour.

3) A chemical that fixes the dye (stops it from running).

4) a) In roller printing, the dye is applied to the surface of a roller which has had the pattern engraved on it. In rotary screen printing, the dye is pressed through holes in a screen that are in the right pattern.
   b) rotary screen printing

Page 37 — Fabric Finishes

1) To change the appearance, texture, wearing properties or after care characteristics of the fabric.

2) The finish could be washed out if the overalls aren't washed correctly.

3) By waterproofing the fabric — mildew will only grow if fabrics made from natural fibres are kept damp.

4) a) Mechanical finishes are finishes that are created by machines.
   b) Mechanical finishes are cheaper to do than chemical finishes.

Page 39 — Components

1) Trouser zips are fixed at one end, but coat zips are not.

2) e.g. parachute clips

3) a) E.g. buttons
   b) E.g. they can fall off.

4) a) They are extra layers of fabric hidden inside a product to give it strength, stability and support.
   b) It can be stuck to fabric by being heated.

Page 41 — Tools and Equipment

1) a) Seam rippers — they're faster than doing it by hand, and won't cut the fabric like scissors could.
   b) Dressmaking scissors (fabric shears).

2) By hand-stitching, with a needle and thread.

3) The thread tension, the stitch type, the stitch length.

4) You could add embroidery. Use CAD software to produce your own designs, which can be transferred to a CAM machine and reproduced accurately.

Page 43 — Computerised Production

1) Computer-Aided Design linked directly to Computer-Aided Manufacture.

2) The cutting is done automatically using the CAD lay-plan, many layers of fabric can be cut at once, and the machine cuts at high speed.

3) Jo can develop her design using CAD and then email it to her client so they can check it's what they want and give their feedback.

4) E.g. fewer people are needed to control the machines, saving on labour costs. CAD/CAM means that higher quality products are produced, which means there's less wastage.

5) E.g. databases are used to help with stock control and spreadsheets are used to work out costs.

Page 45 — Patterns

1) E.g. disassemble an existing product, use a commercial pattern.

2) a) place to fold
   b) dart
   c) buttonhole

3) You can mark the same pattern out on two pieces of fabric at the same time / chalk may rub off.

4) Where patterns for different sizes are laid out on the same fabric sheet.

5) a) e.g. cut pile fabric / striped fabric
   b) e.g. plain-woven fabric with no pattern
   c) non-woven fabric, e.g. felt

Answers

Page 47 — Construction Techniques

1) Fold dart along centre line and pin.
   Stitch along line starting from point.
   Press dart to flatten it. Trim if necessary.

2) Tucks are stitched along the fold.
   Pleats are only secured at the end.

3) Drawstring or zip (they might slip through a buttoned opening)

4) fixed

5) She didn't leave a seam allowance. Duh.

Page 49 — Joining Fabric

1) a) Pinning and tacking/basting

   b) Pinning — advantage: e.g. quick,
      disadvantage: e.g. not very secure/can't check how finished garment will look.

      Tacking — advantage: e.g. secure/can check how finished garment will look.
      disadvantage: e.g. takes time (need to pin first)

2) E.g. they're easy to do / look neat on the outside / can be made to lie flat. But they aren't good at bearing strain / aren't very stretchy.

3) 1.5 cm

4) Use a zigzag stitch for the second line.

5) Place fabric wrong sides together, pin/tack.
   Stitch 8 mm from the edge, then trim down to 3 mm.
   Fold the fabric over so the right sides are together and the seam is on the edge of the fabric.
   Stitch 7 mm from the edge so the raw edge is enclosed.

6) a) double-stitched seam
   b) french seam
   c) overlocked seam

7) Because an overlocker trims at the same time as stitching.

Page 51 — Neatening and Finishing

1) Pinking shears — advantage: quick,
   disadvantage: some fabrics will still fray

   turning edge under — advantage: secure
   disadvantage: takes time/adds bulk

2) Use bias binding to encase the seam allowance on the outside.

3) a) An awkward-shaped edge, such as an armhole or neckline.
   b) Cut a piece of facing about 5 cm wide in the shape of the edge you want to neaten.
      Pin and tack the facing to the product with right sides together. Machine along the seam line.
      Cut notches if necessary.
      Press the facing inside the product and secure with stitches.

4) Look at the size and weight of the product.

5) pressing cloth — protects fabric from the direct heat of the iron.
   sleeve board — sleeves can be slid onto it for ironing.
   tailor's ham — provides a curved surface for ironing, e.g. shoulders.

6) Steam dollies — clothes are put on a body-shaped doll and are inflated with steam to remove creases.

   Tunnel finishers — garments go through a tunnel on hangers. They're steamed and dried in the tunnel to remove creases.

Page 53 — Colouring Fabric

1) a) To even out the colour before dyeing, so that the dyed fabric will be an even colour.
   b) To fix the dye so it won't come out in the wash.

2) a) batik
   b) James could use a fabric made from natural fibres. This would be more absorbent, so would take up the wax and dye better.

3) a) block printing
   b) E.g. he can use the same block to repeat the design many times, but it takes a long time to make the block.

4) She could apply the dye with a diffuser. She could spray the dye more heavily in some areas, and blend colours by spraying them on top of each other.

Page 55 — Decorating Fabric

1) a) appliqué
   b) Two from, e.g: use non-woven fabrics / use a fusible interface like bondaweb / fold the edges under before stitching.

2) a) decoration
   b) E.g. the stitching can be easily damaged.
   c) Iron it and stretch it in an embroidery hoop.
   d) lower/cover feed dogs, replace presser foot with darning foot.

3) Patchwork is attaching small pieces of fabric together to make a bigger piece. Quilting is sandwiching wadding between two pieces of fabric and sewing through all three layers to secure.

Page 57 — Social and Cultural Issues

1) He'll need to design trousers in a longer length.

2) a) E.g. elasticated waistbands / light materials
   b) E.g. fiddly fastenings because older people might find them tricky to do up.

3) E.g. cowboy hats or boots / tartan skirts / tribal patterns / kaftans

4) E.g. transparent fabrics, because some cultures have less revealing dress than others.

Page 59 — Safety and Moral Issues

1) E.g. 'Not suitable for children under 3 years'.

2) Sale and Supply of Goods Act

3) a) Lion Mark
   b) The product meets EU safety standards.

4) Less ethical manufacturers may pay their workers lower wages and spend less on ensuring their workers' safety. This reduces their costs, so they can sell their products more cheaply.

Answers

Page 61 — Environmental Issues

1) Two from, e.g: coal and oil are burned to provide energy used in production / oil is used to make polyester / large amounts of water are used in manufacturing processes.

2) Two from, e.g: recycle waste fabric / reduce packaging / reuse products.

3) They break down the ozone layer in the upper atmosphere, letting in more UV radiation.

4) a) The amount of greenhouse gases released by doing or making something.
   b) Because carbon dioxide is released when they're made and transported. This is because fossil fuels are burned to provide the energy for these processes.
   c) E.g. by using materials that are sourced near to where the product will be manufactured and sold.

5) Two from, e.g: planting trees / investing in wind power / investing in solar power / investing in recycling projects.

Page 63 — Sustainability

1) A resource that will eventually run out.

2) It's where fabrics are reprocessed into fibres which are used to make the same products.

3) E.g. it could be passed on to friends/relatives, given to charity shops, used as a duster.

4) Designing products so that they need replacing after a short amount of time.

5) E.g. recycle — she could use fabric that is recyclable or recycled,
   repair — she could include spare beads and thread that could be used to mend the cushion, etc.

Page 65 — Production Methods

1) E.g. high labour costs (because highly-skilled workers are needed and things take a long time to make), greater material costs (because materials are high quality and bought in small quantities).

2) Batch production is when a specific number of identical products are made.

3) There are times when no product is being made, e.g. when machines are being set up for a different batch.

4) Batch production is good for making t-shirts because batches can be made to fill specific orders and the machines can be easily changed to make different colours/sizes/styles of t-shirt.

5) Economy of scale is where the cost of producing each item gets lower the more of it you produce.

6) People who can afford it are prepared to pay more for a unique garment that has been designed to their exact requirements and which fits them perfectly.

Page 67 — Quality Control

1) a) Performs its function well
      Looks good and attracts consumers
   b) Has been made to a good standard
      Is accurate to the original design

2) Materials — e.g. quality baby clothes must be durable so it's important to choose a hardwearing fabric, e.g. cotton.
   Processes — e.g. quality baby clothes must be comfortable to wear so they should use a French seam that covers any rough fabric edges that might irritate the skin.

3) 105 mm (± 5)

4) Accuracy is important to ensure that the final product is of a high quality and has no defects, like sleeves of different lengths or buttons not lining up.

5) Raw materials are checked to make sure they are correct and in good condition. A final prototype or sample is made to make sure that the manufacturing process is correct and the design criteria have been met. Production samples will be checked at several stages during production to make sure the quality is good and the product still matches the design specification. The completed product will also be checked.

Page 69 — Labelling

1) fibre content

2) advantage — removes stains more effectively.
   disadvantage — can cause some fabrics to change shape.

3) They should be reshaped and laid out flat while damp. This is so they don't stretch.

4) Radio frequency identification (RFID) labels have a computer chip in them. The computer chip stores information about the product and is read by a receiver using radio waves. The labels can be read from a distance and lots of labels can be read at once. This means a stock control system can be updated as soon as the goods arrive at the store or warehouse.

Page 71 — Health and Safety

1) A risk assessment identifies potential hazards and the precautions that should be put in place to minimise the risks.

2) Using tools and equipment, using materials and chemicals, correct protective clothing, safe working practices.

3) Wear rubber gloves and goggles, ensure adequate fume extraction/ventilation.

4) E.g:
   Stitching fingers / eye injuries — use machine guards.
   Inhalation of textile dust — use dust extractors and have adequate ventilation.
   Getting long hair trapped in machine — use hair nets or tie hair back.
   Injuries from being knocked — ensure adequate space around work area.
   Hearing damage from noisy machines — wear ear protection.

Index

<u>Index</u>